Your Prosperity Paradigm

11 Steps to Creating & Living a Super Successful Life

By Leslie Fieger

Your Prosperity Paradigm

Copyright © 2008 by Leslie Fieger

All rights reserved. No part of this book may be reproduced or transmitted in any form nor by any means, electronic, mechanical, photographic or phonographic process; nor may it be stored in any retrieval system, or otherwise copied for public or private use - other than for "fair use" as brief quotations embodied in articles or reviews –without prior written permission of the copyright holder and publisher.

The author of this book does not dispense medical or psychological advice or suggest the use of any technique as a form of treatment for physical, emotional or mental problems without the advice of a licensed physician, therapist or health care practitioner either directly or indirectly. The intent of the author is only to offer information of a general nature to assist the reader in the personal quest for material, physical, emotional, mental and spiritual well-being. In the event that you, the reader, choose to exercise your right to use any of the information in this book, the author and his agents assume no liability for your actions.

ISBN 978-0-557-47767-8

Other books by Leslie Fieger include:

Alexandra's DragonFire

The Master Key

Awakenings

The Delfin Trilogy, which consists of…

The Initiation
The Journey
The Quest

All are available at http://www.lulu.com/lf2 or through http://www.LeslieFieger.ca

Also see page 163 of this book for more information on each of the above mentioned books.

This book is dedicated to my parents, Audrey and Al Fieger, who brought me into this world, gave me so great a head start on the adventure, were there to support me when I stumbled, celebrated my successes and are still my cheerleaders. My parents are my heroes.

They grew up during the great depression and were able to come out of that difficult time, forge a path for themselves and build a life of substance, plus create an attitude of open ended possibilities for their nine children.

Amongst the hundreds of books in my house, as I was growing up, were such success classics as Napoleon Hill's *Think and Grow Rich*, Dale Carnegie's *How to Win Friends and Influence People* and even that great LP recording from Earl Nightingale, *The Strangest Secret*.

I also grew up listening to Harry Belafonte sing *The Banana Boat Song* "Come Mr. Tally man, tally me banana…" and other calypso songs.

It is no wonder I now live in the Caribbean and write books about creating success.

Thanks Al and Audrey for everything.

This book is also dedicated to you, the reader. I hope it serves you.

Your Prosperity Paradigm

11 Steps to Creating & Living a Super Successful Life

Introduction: A Masterpiece	9
Chapter One: Envisioneering Your Reality	17
Chapter Two: Falling In Love	33
Chapter Three: Living On Purpose	45
Chapter Four: Seeing Beyond The Veil	61
Chapter Five: Living In Grace	71
Chapter Six: Playing By The Rules	83
Chapter Seven: Charting The Course	101
Chapter Eight: Speaking The Truth	115
Chapter Nine: Acting The Part	125
Chapter Ten: Following Your Bliss	133
Chapter Eleven: Mirror, Mirror	145
Epilogue: The Formula	159
Appendix: Maslow's Hierarchy of Needs	161
More from Leslie Fieger	163

Introduction

Your Masterpiece

It is not my objective, in these pages, to merely inspire and/or motivate you to create success and fulfillment. It is, rather, my intention to supply you with the methodology to actually create that success and find that fulfillment. I think that the desire to have more success is already latent in your heart and the ideal of greater personal fulfillment lies dormant in your mind.

I believe that it is an inherent and important aspect of human nature to want to be, to do and to have more. It is this intrinsic urge that has brought us from being simple proto-humans searching for daily sustenance to becoming advanced intellectual creatures who are capable of building orbiting space stations, defining the human genetic code, creating previously unimagined wealth and so much more.

This same urge that drove Alexander and Napoleon, Michelangelo and Shakespeare, Isaac Newton and Albert Einstein, Andrew Carnegie and Richard Branson, Marco Polo and Ferdinand Magellan, is as natural a part of your personality as is the urge to procreate.

I also believe that, although we each innately desire to be, to do and to have more, we are each, unfortunately, largely constrained (limited) in our ability to achieve this "more" by our existing paradigms.

A paradigm, as I use the term here, is a set of experiences, beliefs, values and assumptions that affect the way an individual perceives reality and responds to that perception.

In other words, **your assumed and unexamined personal beliefs and individual predominant methods of thinking may actually be holding you back from fulfilling your potential to self-actualize and to create massive personal success.**

Since we are, each of us, limited by our assumed paradigms; in order to reach these higher levels of attainment, achievement, accomplishment and fulfillment that we desire, we need to decide to let go of these limiting mindsets and somehow figure out how to adopt more allowing and enabling belief systems.

Each person who desires to self-actualize needs to learn and apply a new Prosperity Paradigm in order to be all that he is capable of being, to do all that she is capable of doing in order to have all that he desires to have in order to maximize her experience of, and enjoyment of, the great gift of being alive on Planet Earth.

More importantly, each of us cannot fulfill our purpose to be contributory to the future of our species unless we maximize our individual capacity to be, to do and to have more of what is available to us.

Since what is available to us is only limited by our own imaginations, we each need to expand our ability to imagine and to train ourselves to expect so much more. Our ability to imagine is defined (limited) by our paradigms. Want more? Change your paradigm!

This book was written to empower you to free yourself from the mental and emotional limitations (that you may not even be aware of having) that are holding you back from being, doing and having all that you desire and deserve to be, do and have. And, much more importantly… to free yourself from the mental chains that may very well be preventing you from getting the joy, personal fulfillment and empowerment from your already existing, but under-appreciated, achievements.

I have a profound faith in the potential of the human creature to not only evolve naturally over time, both as a species and as individuals; but also to take intentional control of our own personal evolution and self-fulfillment in order to radically transform our lives in any given moment.

At the very least, those of us who are fortunate enough to have satisfied the first two levels of basic human needs as identified by Abraham Maslow (see Appendix 1), are free, if we choose, to undertake the journey to conscious self-actualization; and as such, are capable of creating both a spectacular immediate success for ourselves and a valuable lasting legacy for our fellows.

Of course, you can be willing to change, to transform yourself, in order to have that more that you imagine is possible; but you also need a bit more than just the intense desire and the profound willingness. You also need the system that will take you there. You need the defined technology. You need the proven path to follow.

I am going to assume that, since you have read this far, you have the willingness, the desire and, maybe even, the commitment that is necessary to undertake this change in paradigms from scarcity to abundance, from paucity to prosperity. And that, perhaps the only thing you lack is the proven methodology of personal transformation (or technology of success) that will take you from where you are to where you want to go.

If so, please continue to read on; because in the pages that follow is the time-tested, proven and very real system that has produced enormous success for tens of thousands of other people, who, just like you, decided to take control of their own lives and of their own success and happiness. All that you need to do now in order to make it work for you, as it has for so many people before you, is to actually apply it to the way you live your life, day-by-day and moment-by-moment.

There is an old saying that goes something like... "You can feed a man for a day by giving him a fish; but you can feed a man for a lifetime by teaching him how to fish." True enough, potentially, but the sad bigger truth is that you can teach a man how to fish, but he will still starve if he does not actually go fishing. The trained fisherman who sits on the beach and stares at the sea will still go hungry.

The knowledge that you need to create the success you desire is here in these pages. However, the application of this knowledge is entirely up to you. Only you can make it real. It is always up to you to launch the boat, put to sea and drop your lines in the ocean of pure potential.

This knowledge of how to create success is not theoretical. It has been proven over and over again by the direct application of so many people. This is not a hypothetical philosophy. This is not some empty motivation. It is a very real and applicable technology. It is up to you to put it to use to construct the life of your dreams, like so many before you have already done. Will you? Only you can make that choice.

No matter what we each do in life... homemaker, business person, architect, engineer, painter, author... our own life is our greatest work of art. We can, by the choices we make, either create an original masterpiece or an unremarkable paint-by-numbers piece.

Each of us has the potential to create a wondrous masterpiece; yet so many people end up with the off-the-shelf art, the velvet painting version of life, simply because they don't have the tools needed to create the masterpiece. That is sad.

What is even sadder is when those people who do have the necessary tools do not use them, or use them poorly.

A hammer and chisel are two simple tools. Almost anyone can use them to break apart a marble floor. Michelangelo used these same tools to create the glorious Statue of David, the sublime Pieta and many other great works of art.

The tools and techniques that you need to create a masterpiece of success for yourself are right here in this book. I urge you to put them to use. They will produce results. If your intention is clear, your resolve is firm, your ideal is grand and your desire is strong enough, you can use these tools to create that great work of art called a happy, successful, fulfilling and contributory life.

It is possible that you may have previously read, heard or come across some, or all, of the ideas, tools and techniques you will find in these pages.

Almost everyone has the same tendency when they come across some familiar information: they say to themselves, "oh yeah, I already know that," and they then stop reading, stop listening, skip over or dismiss the idea.

So, yes, even though you may be familiar with some of the ideas in this book, I urge you to read it slowly, completely and carefully. Perhaps, even more than one time. Familiarity with something does NOT denote knowledge of something. You demonstrate your knowledge by your application of it.

For example, you can read a recipe for lasagna in a cookbook; you can listen to your grandma tell you how to make it; you can even tell when you are eating a good lasagna or a mediocre one. But you will not know how to cook a great lasagna until you get into the kitchen and use the tools and apply the recipe. It is the application that denotes true knowledge and understanding rather than mere familiarity.

You may be familiar with the recipe for success, but unless you have already created all the success you desire to have, you either have not applied the information to the way you live your life; or, you have not practiced it enough to create that great lasagna (success).

So, please read the formula/recipe again, even if you think that you are familiar with it. You may have missed some critical nuance (like that teaspoon of oregano) that is a necessary component.

Enjoy your reading. May it taste better than the best lasagna you've ever eaten. Once you've read this recipe, get into the kitchen and start cooking up your very own success story. Make the application; create your masterpiece.

"Dream lofty dreams, and as you dream, so you shall become. Your vision is the promise of what you shall one day be; your ideal is the prophecy of what you shall at last unveil."

~ James Allen

"Most people are not really free. They are confined by the niche in the world that they carve out for themselves. They limit themselves to fewer possibilities by the narrowness of their vision."

~ V.S. Naipaul

Chapter One

Envisioneering Your Reality

You may not have heard the word "envisioneering" before; but it is a great word. It is a great word because it describes how powerful you are when you align yourself with the scientific processes that the universe uses to make things manifest.

Envisioneering is a combination of envision and engineering. To envision means "to create a picture in one's own mind or imagination"; and engineering means "the application of science and mathematics by which the properties of matter and the sources of energy in nature are made useful to people" (Webster).

So, envisioneering means: Using the laws governing matter and energy to take a vision from pure imagination and to make it real (realize it) in the everyday world.

Of course, the very first step in getting what you desire is to actually decide exactly what it is that you desire.

Strangely enough, most people do not do that very well. People will say they want success or happiness or wealth, (which are really quite nebulous terms unless and until they are clearly defined), but they don't actually know what they mean because they have not defined them enough for them to be personally meaningful.

Over the years, I have spent considerable time mentoring and coaching people about how to create wealth. One of the very first questions I ask people that I mentor is "what does wealthy mean to you?" Not one in ten people have thought enough about it to actually be able to define it for themselves, let alone precisely explain to me what the word wealthy means to them.

It is not up to me to define what wealthy means to you or anyone else; and, in fact, being or feeling wealthy is very variable. Each person has different standards and expectations. Having one million dollars in the bank might enable many people to feel quite wealthy; but I can assure you that if Donald Trump was reduced to having only a meager million dollars in his bank account, he would feel quite impoverished.

I have a holistic general definition that I offer people, which is that "wealth is an abundance of physical, emotional, mental, spiritual and material well-being." It is, however, up to each person to specify what wealth means to themselves. It is up to you to define your own success. If you allow others to do it for you, or if you assume some societal standard, then you will forever be wearing hand-me-down ideals that will not quite fit.

The other major problem that people seem to have with deciding exactly what it is that they desire to have (in addition to lack of specificity) is that they often describe what they say they want by what they don't want. For example… most people I ask to define financial freedom (which is one of the ways they answer my request to get more specific about what wealth means to them) say that it is freedom from debt and money concerns. They don't want debt and they don't want to be concerned about money. But what do they actually want? Don't know. Can't say.

Before you even begin the process of creating success in any area of your life, whether it be your intimate personal relationship or your material abundance, you must very clearly decide and specifically define exactly what it is that you desire to have. Define it by what it is and so not define it by what it is not. If you define it by what it is not, your attention will be forever focused on its opposite and you will tend to continue to create that opposite rather than the actual thing or effect desired.

If you truly want to be wealthy, I strongly suggest that you stop and define your success this very day. At the end of this chapter, you will find some exercises to help you in this process.

The beginning of any intentionally created event or circumstance in your life is to first create the ideal in your imagination.

Embellish it with all the details and clarity you can muster. Feel and affirm its reality in order to build your belief muscle. Visualize it in its completeness. Support its veracity with vision boards, written affirmations and by designing specific plans to effectuate its realization. Keep your attention focused on this imagined ideal and do not allow any current outside events and circumstances to distract you from its reality.

Remind yourself that whatever can be conceived in imagination and believed in wholeheartedly, can invariably be achieved, if you take the necessary steps in accordance with certain tried and true principles. All wealth is the product of a creative, directed and intentional consciousness.

The future is a blank slate. Peter Drucker once commented that the best way to predict the future is to create it. It is the visionaries who create the future. If you want to be in control of how your life turns out, you need to become a visionary and practice envisioneering. Your imagination is the creative workshop in which you construct your reality.

It never ceases to amaze me. Almost everyone peers into the future through a rear-view mirror. The future is imagined as a continuation of the past. I suppose there is a certain security in that; much like a padded cell. Hardly anyone practices creative envisioneering.

To be an envisioneer, you must first have the courage to look into the future with the recognition that there is nothing there yet, except that which you imagine; and then, the force of will to imagine a personal ideal; and then, the impertinence to believe that the imagined ideal is real. In fact, you see it as being more real than all that has come before or exists in this present moment. In short, you must be an idealist.

Each of us, unfortunately, is educated to be a realist, to deal with things as they are, to see the world as it is and to 'realistically' go about making our way within what already exists. In other words, we are trained to be creatures of event and circumstance.

Those who decide to shape events and circumstances to match what they envision are the idealists. They end up as the movers and shakers, the leaders, the ones who create personal success, cultural innovation, the future and also, ultimately, history as well. The average employee is a realist. The entrepreneur is an idealist. A realist is a creature of event and circumstance; an idealist is a creator of event and circumstance.

Each of us may aspire, in our hearts, to be prosperous, to be fulfilled, to live a life of purpose and passion. However, living life as a realist makes it almost impossible to succeed in achieving these ideals. If you are to have any hope of making real your ideals, you must learn to become an idealist and to practice the art of creative envisioneering,

The main contrast between the realist and the idealist is that the realist sees with his eyes open and the idealist sees most clearly with his eyes closed. The realist believes in the explicate outer world; the idealist knows that the explicate is derived from the implicate inner world of creative imagination, that the physical arises from the metaphysical; that all that is created is first imagined. Realists rely upon the definite. Idealists rely upon the infinite.

It is often said that idealists are out of touch with (physical) reality. But, it is the realists who are the ones who are out of touch with the greater (metaphysical) reality; and idealists are the ones who mold and shape their own, and our collective, future reality. They are envisioneers; creating the future they imagine; living their dreams; enacting their inner vision; using metaphysical principles to form and fashion the physical actualities they desire.

Idealists (envisioneers) create the future that the realists end up (by default) living in, having no choice but to cope with the existing reality, while the envisioneer is still busily creating a new dream. If you want to live the life of your own dreams, you must become an envisioneer and learn to ignore the comfortable constraints of reality.

The envisioneer has taught himself to believe in what can be imagined more than in what is temporarily existent in the external world.

Do you want more out of life? Envision more. Become a dreamweaver. Start imagining the possibilities that lie open to you. Start believing in your own power to imagine an ideal and then to make it real.

Of course, you must begin from where you are presently at. Where else can you start from? So, there is no point in denying your current situation. It is, after all, the result of your previous method of thinking; the result of your previous way of being and behaving in the world, the result of your existing paradigms.

However, there is no reason at all to expect that the future will unfold as the past has happened, or even as the present exists, except that you imagine that it will. That is, if you are prepared to imagine something else, something bigger and better, something that actually fills your heart and mind with joy and excitement.

I like to remind everyone that everything (and I mean *everything*, including your own concept about who you are, why you are alive and what you are capable of doing) exists entirely in your own imagination. That is often a difficult concept for people to 'grok' (understand at a soul level); but it is nevertheless true.

Your entire everyday reality (and your whole perception of the universe) is constructed entirely in your imagination in each moment, filtered through your belief systems and ingrained ways of thinking about reality and your emotional entrainments.

A quick aside… as a writer, I don't like to use the same word twice in the same sentence if there is a viable alternative, so I checked on synonyms for reality and found that "idealism" is considered an antonym. That just proves the pervasive societal prejudice (meme/paradigm) against imagination and idealization as reality generator.

The great good news is that, if everything exists entirely in your imagination, then you can imagine, idealize, visualize, envision anything you define and desire to be true for you, and it can become true.

The universe is not some machine or mechanically unfolding process that was created billions of years ago during the event typically called the Big Bang. It is an evolving living entity seeking self-expression and self-actualization and it is continuously re-creating itself each quantum moment.

This is a critical understanding; not just for cosmologists and quantum physicists - it is critical for anyone who wants to come into a full understanding and application of their creative power. If you want to be able to create the ideal events and circumstances of your individual life, you need to know how the universe is created anew in each new moment.

You are you; an individual, complete unto yourself... a Holon. But, you exist within and are inseparable from the whole, universe. Your existence is governed by the same rules that govern the existence of the universe. Your ability to be consciously creative is enhanced by knowing and applying the universal creative process.

The universe blinks in and out of existence each and every moment; it goes on and off; it recreates itself. This all happens at the sub-quantum level, so you are not normally aware of it.

When you observe (perceive) the universe, even your little corner of it, you tend to think of it as a continuous, moving process... like a movie. But just like a movie, there may be the illusion of a seamless continuity, but the reality is more like a series of still images strung together to produce movement and momentum.

In a movie, the individual frames run at 24 per second, too fast for the eye to capture the individual images so that they all **seem** to run together to produce the illusion of one continuous moving picture. The actuality is that a movie is a series of still shots, each one being just a little different than the one before.

At the quantum level of universe, the process is exactly the same except that the individual frames run at billions per second... a very high frequency. In fact, there are billions of different frequencies, all acting in a grand harmony, to create the moving picture of a temporal and spatial universe.

So, when you look out your window and see the leaves of a tree moving in the breeze, what you are seeing is a series of individual snap shots strung together to produce the illusion of leaf movement, each snap shot somewhat different than the previous one as the various fermions, bosons, photons and imaginatons flash in and out of existence.

(Imaginaton is a word I made up. Just as a photon is a basic wave/particle of light, an imaginaton is a basic wave/particle of thought energy.)

So what, you might wonder, is the relevance of this to your life and how it unfolds. Everything! Whether you are ignorant of, or aware of, how universe (and everything in it including you) is re-created anew each moment, you are still a participant. You can choose to be a passive participant (like you imagine a rock to be) or you can choose to be an active participant THEREBY actually influencing how the next quantum snapshot turns out.

Yes, such is your power. Here's how it works.

All this blinking on and off, the frequency of the master vibration, is subject to the various interplays of the innumerable sub-frequencies of the various vibrations of the individual parts of universe (all Holons in their own right).

The Pacific Ocean, for allegorical example, is made up of various little wavelets. If you toss a pebble from the shore, you create a new set of waves and the whole behavior of the ocean changes. You may not notice it, but it does. Say the pebble is an asteroid that slams into the ocean from space, you might then notice? Well, sure you would. Just ask the dinosaurs.

Ok, now you have the concept. The universe is a vast sea of vibration made up of various little (and not so little) interference patterns caused by the various frequencies when they interact. These interference patterns are the snapshots that make the movie. Interject a new waveform (toss in a pebble) and you change the interference pattern and the next snap shot is changed. Keep on doing it and you change the whole future picture.

Your thoughts and your emotions which are determined your beliefs/paradigms are your vibratory output. This vibratory output exists within the universe. It also affects universe. Your vibratory output creates interference patterns in the quantum ocean of universe. So what?

Well, if you want to change the behavior of the universe, then change your personal vibratory output: change your thoughts, change your emotions, change your beliefs.

You might well say that your little vibrations will not have much effect on the whole BIG universe, but then, you really don't want to change the universe all that much do you? I mean, you don't want to change the orbit of the earth or anything even remotely like that, do you? You just want to change a few very small things like the events and circumstances of your life.

Back to the seashore… you go to the beach, the sea is dead calm today, smooth as glass. You jump in, splashing and making all kinds of commotion. Your little immediate area of the Pacific is no longer calm; it is turbulent. Sand is stirred up, fish scatter, froth and bubbles are everywhere in your immediate vicinity.

Ripples spread out, the little waves you make even rush up against the beach destroying a child's sand castle built too close to the water's edge. The young girl who was floating on her back with eyes closed in the calm sea a moment before is now having water from your waves splashed into her face. You have changed reality.

Your mental and emotional output creates a commotion in your immediate environment and changes the reality you are experiencing. Change the nature of that commotion and you change the reality picture of your immediate environment. Maintain a consistent mental and emotional pattern and you have a long lasting affect on your immediate environment. Keep it up consistently for a long time and you will even change the whole ocean.

Let's leave the seashore and return to our movie set.

You have 24 still frames passing by each second. Let's say that all of them except frame #2 in a one second snapshot is exactly the same as the other 23, what do you end up seeing? No movement, no change. Now, take a one-minute sequence, that's 1,440 separate frames. In second two of this sequence, frame 3 is different but all 23 other frames remain the same; in second three, frame

4 is different but the rest remain the same and so on until you come to second #59 and frame 60 is different and the rest remain the same. What do you end up with at the end of one minute? 60 different frames spread out amongst 1380 identical ones producing some minor illusion of movement but with an unchanged overall picture.

This is how everyday normal passive participation in universe creates your reality picture. You actually have about 60,000 thoughts per day; but, 99% of them are the same old repetitive subconscious self-talk and ingrained patterns of thinking, believing and feeling.

Occasionally throughout the day you think about your hopes and ambitions or focus on your goals or think specific thoughts related to your life's purpose, but most of the frames remain the same. You end up with the illusion of movement and an unchanged reality picture.

You attend some seminar and your thinking patterns change for a few days and you even notice some changes in your life, but soon, you revert to your habitual way of random, unintentional thoughts, emotions and beliefs and no lasting change happens in your life.

As the universe blinks in and out of existence, it takes all that happens in one moment to re-create the next. Your individual thoughts, emotions and beliefs are in this mix. If you have a unique thought one moment and then for the next 10, revert to habit (same old), you do not notice there was a snap shot of universe that was different, but it was.

If you hold clear, consistent, intentional thoughts entwined with clear, consistent, intentional emotions from moment to moment and when universe blinks in and out of existence, these specifically chosen new thoughts, emotions and beliefs will change enough frames in the sequence of snap shots for you to actually perceive the different universe you have created; at least, your little corner of the universe… the events and circumstances of your life.

So, there it is. Simple, yet elegant and profound. Your thoughts shape your reality. If you want a different reality, change your thinking, your old belief patterns and your limiting paradigms. Imagine more!

Since there are more than 6 billion other humans occupying this planet right now, all of them thinking and thus producing effects, you are, to some degree, somewhat limited in what you can create. The realm of possibilities is restricted by the group mindset… what Jung called the Collective Unconscious and Sheldrake called Morphic Resonance and Dawkins called the Meta-Meme.

Fortunately, since the idea of success already exists within the cultural meme set, you can create your individual success by thinking the right kind of thoughts and by creating and focusing your attention on the ideals you create in your imagination without having to change the whole paradigm of humanity; just your own paradigm about prosperity, abundance and wealth.

I define prosperity as being the abundance of all things held ideal in mind and dear in heart. Your job is to figure out what you are holding in mind (as an ideal) and in heart (as a desire) and to decide to hold bigger and better ideals and desires AND to consider them as real and true, despite any seeming evidence to the contrary. That is envisioneering. It is a very real science and a very effective technology.

You can study the science of success for years and years until you become an expert and still not have the success you desire until you actually take action by making the application; and as I said earlier in this chapter, you can only start from where you presently are at.

The chart below will assist you to do the honest self-analysis to determine where you are at, decide perhaps where you want to get to (your ideal) and how to get there. Obviously your answers will not fit in the space provided. I have provided you the opportunity to look at your wealth holistically by including all 5 aspects of your beingness. As we continue through the book, you will have more opportunities to expand your lists and the currently empty rows in this chart will show more opportunities for new insights on your part.

You have heard it before, but it bears repeating… it is insane to continue being (thinking, feeling and believing) and doing the same old things and somehow expecting different results. In order to transform your world, you must first transform yourself. Start that process by creating and defining your ideals.

Quick Review:

That piece of advice so often given, "be realistic" is bad advice. Idealists create the world in which realists get to live. Create the vision of your ideal world in your imagination and use it as the light that shines into the dark unknown of your future to illuminate your purpose and passion.

The focus of your attention will determine the results that you get to live with moment-by-moment and day-by-day. No clear ideals and no focus means that your life will happen by default rather than by design.

The quantum world is malleable to your will. Your thoughts, feelings, beliefs and intentions shape your reality by influencing how quantum wave forms behave. Everything is energy and energy is everything.

Direct Action Steps:

First, write down your own definition of success. Don't just make a list of things you'd like to have. Describe exactly what you would need to become, to be doing and to have in order to feel successful. Success means different things to different people. What exactly does it mean to you? How can you possibly become successful if you don't even know what it means?

Next, write down your personal ideals. Make this list holistic. Include all aspects of your self: material, physical, emotional, mental and spiritual. It may take you some time to contemplate and arrive at an honest and complete listing of your ideals. It took me a full week of tough work to get clear about what were my personal ideals; rather than allowing myself to adopt some supposed or imposed listing of societal expectations. The following chart may help you in the process.

	Material & Financial	Physical & Environmental	Emotional & Relationship	Mental & Educational	Spiritual & Ethical
Your defined ideals					
Your current situation					
Distance from					

ideal					
Planned arrival date					

"If there is no passion in your life, then have you really lived? Find your passion, whatever it may be. Become it, and let it become you and you will find great things happen for you, to you and because of you."

~ Alan Armstrong

Without passion man is a mere latent force and possibility, like the flint which awaits the shock of the iron before it can give forth its spark."

~ Henri-Frédéric Amiel

Chapter Two

Falling in Love

So, you have now created that perfect and wondrously clearly defined ideal in your imagination. Congratulations. You have just thought something into being. You are becoming an envisioneer and a conscious creator of the circumstances of your own life.

The creative power of intentional thought is the most important discovery ever made by humanity; and, when an individual human being makes the decision to begin to think on purpose, she begins the process of self-mastery which will take her from being a mere creature of event and circumstance to becoming a creator of event and circumstance.

You should know, however, that, as important as your thoughts are in the creative process, your emotions are even more important.

Your emotions and feelings are important for two reasons: the first is that they are a guidance system that tells you if you are on track; the second is that the creative power of thought is multiplied many times when a specific and strong emotional current is attached to the thought or ideal.

Let's deal with the second aspect first (just for fun).

When a profoundly held, passionate feeling is attached to an ideal (which is just a consistent thought form held in mind), one of the most basic laws of the universe begins to act on your behalf. That natural law, which is always in operation, is usually called The Law of Attraction.

This law defines that "like energy is attracted to like energy." You can easily recognize it in action in the physical universe as the forces called gravity and electromagnetism. Both are invisible forces. Invisible they may be, but without them, our universe would not exist. That is how important and powerful they are. As invisible and intangible as the energy of emotion may be, it is also extremely powerful.

Your passionate desire for your ideals and goals will attract the people and resources you need to effectuate or make real your ideal. You should already have seen and recognized that passionate people attract other people to their cause. (Because there is also a Law of Polarity, sometimes these ideals also repel people... those who are not aligned with their ideal and would not, therefore, contribute to its realization.)

You may not, however, have yet consciously recognized that resources are also attracted to a passionate desire combined with a clear ideal. Resources like money, systems and opportunities are also drawn to the harmonious energetic output called passion. Sometimes it seems like magic how those people who have the drive, the desire, the ideal are lucky enough to fall into situations where it all comes so easily to them. Now you know why. It is The Law of Attraction in action.

Now, you may not yet know that your emotional output is energy and that you broadcast this energy at all times; but nevertheless, it is a scientific fact. You have even recognized or felt this energy. Have you ever walked into a room where there was an extremely angry person?

Even before they said anything, you felt the bad vibes. They are broadcasting this energetic output like a radio station broadcasts radio waves. Have you ever been at a rock concert and felt the waves of energy flowing between crowd and performer? Same thing: emotional energy being emitted by people.

Like energy is attracted to like energy. That is the way things work. You stay on this planet, even though it is spinning at 1,000 miles per hour and produces a huge amount of centrifugal force entirely because "like energy is attracted to like energy". (Your mass is attracted to the Earth's mass. They are vibrationally and energetically alike).

The things that show up in your life show up because of what you think and what you emote. What you think and how you feel is your energetic output. It is really simple: you attract what is most alike or in alignment with how you are being energetically.

Have you ever noticed that people who are afraid of being victimized end up being victimized? It is the same Law of Attraction in action. Fear is powerful; so powerful that wolves can smell it and sharks can sense it from miles away. You may fake being brave, but your fear is pouring out of you like a big signal from one of those super radio stations. It attracts that which is attracted to that form of energy, what is most aligned with it. You've seen it in print before, "What you fear shall come upon you." Fortunately it is not fear alone that creates results.

The four most consciously powerful ways of feeling that will bring to you those things that are held ideal in mind and dear in heart are: Desire, Passion, Gratitude and Joy. In fact, the secret of enacting The Law of Attraction to work on your behalf is to:

1- Attach a fervent desire to a clearly defined and consistently held ideal

2- Be passionate about your life and your ideals.
3- Feel grateful for the multitude of blessings you already have and that you will have in your life.
4- Be joyful. Enjoy being alive. Enjoy having the things you have.

Desire is the metaphysical equivalent of gravity. It draws things of like vibration together as surely as gravity draws hydrogen molecules together to form stars and holds planets in orbit around stars.

Unfortunately, many people are incapable of allowing themselves to feel the intense desire necessary to enact the Law of Attraction in any discernable way. We have all been cultural trained to suppress our desires rather than express them. In Western civilization desire is treated as a sin. In Eastern cultures desire is said to be the source of all suffering. Both of these erroneous memes or paradigms serve to prevent individuals from becoming the powerful creators that they are capable of becoming. Your capacity to feel intense desire is a divine characteristic. Your ability to attach desire to an ideal amplifies your personal creative power.

The sub-quantum wave form of potentiality is collapsed into an actuality by the energetic output of the observer/participant. You become a creator of your own reality by collapsing the infinite potentialities inherent in universe by your energetic output, which is composed of the combination of thought and emotion. Create the ideal and make it as clear and precise as you can, attach the desire and make it as intense as you can and you empower yourself to transform your world.

Desire engenders passion. Passionate people are exciting, charismatic and attractive. Passion is both infective and effective. Passionate people enroll other people into assisting them in achieving their ideals. Be passionate about your life and your ideals and others will support you just to feel your passion, your energy, your enthusiasm, your fire.

Passion is the fire that lights your path and fuels your commitment as you walk into a future of your own creation.

Passion also enables you to feel more alive. In fact, you **are** more alive when you are passionate about something, such as that ideal you have envisioned for yourself. A life without passion is not a life, it is merely an existence. Envision that ideal. Become passionate about it. If the ideal you have set for yourself does not engender your profound passion, it is not the right ideal. Choose or create another one that does kindle your passion to ignite and burn bright.

I'll talk about gratitude and joy in other chapters at some length, so I'll skip those other two aspects of using feelings to utilize the Law of Attraction for now.

Let's look now at that first reason why your feelings are so important to the creation of your ideal.

Your feelings are an internal guide that tells you if you are following the right path. If what you are doing feels enjoyable, then you are on track. Keep going. However, if what you are doing feels distressing, then you have allowed yourself to become distracted from what is important to your personal fulfillment and success and have strayed from your path.
Yes, occasionally, you may feel frustrated or uncomfortable as you pursue your ideal. I love to hike up mountains and there has been many an occasion when I felt that I had reached the limits of my endurance and felt

like quitting; but when I forced my mind to focus on the ideal (the top of that ridge) and remembered that awesome feeling of exhilaration that comes from being at the top, I was able to continue on and reach the top. It was the thoughts of quitting that saddened me. As soon as I re-focused my attention on what was important, rather than the tired legs and lungs, I was able to feel good again about the strenuous effort.

So, when I say that your feelings are your internal guide that informs you if you are on your right path, I am not speaking about momentary and fleeting emotions, but of those pervasive feelings of despondency or uselessness or malaise that last hours or days. These feelings are clear indications that you are not on your true path to success, happiness, fulfillment and prosperity.

Remember that I define wealth as a holistic and harmonious blend of physical, emotional, mental, spiritual and material well-being. If your emotional well-being is quite obviously not there, then you need to do some serious self-examination to determine how it is that you have gone astray and then figure out what you need to do to get back on track with being in sync with your defined ideals.

The title of this chapter is Falling In Love. I think you can see now that **one of the major secrets to consciously creating a successful and fulfilling life is to learn to fall in love with your ideal,** having an intense desire for its actualization and being hyper-passionate about its value.

Moreover, your life will be so much more rewarding and filled with ease and success if you learn to fall in love with life itself, with you yourself and with the enormous potential you have to continuously self-actuate and create whatever you can imagine and believe in as real and true.

Both ancient proven metaphysics and modern quantum physics tell us that our personal vibratory output influences how things unfold in our reality picture. Your thoughts and your feelings are, like everything else in the physical universe, energy as defined by vibration. Your personal vibratory output (a mix of thoughts and feelings) interacts with the pre-existing background matrix of universal vibratory output to create an interference pattern. That interference pattern is what you perceive with your consciousness (your attention) when you look at your world.

Since you can consciously choose what to think and how to feel, you can change your personal vibratory output and hence change the interference pattern that is created when your vibratory output interferes with the universal. That field of influence is relatively small in the universal scheme of things, but it is big enough to actually determine how the events and circumstances of your life unfold.

Although there is a huge variety and subtlety to human emotional experience, all emotions are a subset of two primary ways of feeling. One is fear and the other is love. Both are extremely powerful and creative. Desire and passion, along with joy and gratitude, compassion, happiness, etc are aspects of the emotion of love. Distress, worry, hate, anger, anxiety and disgust are aspects of the emotion of fear.
Both fear and love work to attract to you the thing that the emotion is attached to. Hating war creates conflict. Loving peace creates harmony. Unfortunately there are also some people who love war and that passion creates more war. Also, unfortunately there are some people who also know how to engender fear in the populace in

order to control their responses and limit their ability to be self-reliant and consciously creative. If you have learned to prefer security over freedom and safety over opportunity, you are motivated mostly by fear. Is that truly how you wish to live?

Anxiety about debt creates more debt. Passion for prosperity creates more prosperity. Fear of failure leads to failure. Love of success leads to success.

Just as you are not normally aware of 99% of the 60,000 thoughts you think each day until and unless you decide to pursue personal mastery and begin examining how you are thinking and why you think what you think, you probably do not normally pay attention to how you are feeling in most moments and whether or not that feeling is one of love or fear. To help you achieve some clarity, I have listed the most common feelings.

If you are feeling any of the things in the following list, then you are coming from the emotion of love: adoration, affection, fondness, liking, caring, compassion, desire, passion, joy, bliss, delight, gratitude, gladness, happiness, ecstasy, pride, zeal, exhilaration, pleasure, contentment, hope, optimism, enthrallment, amazement, euphoria, jubilation or rapture.

If you are feeling any of the things in the following list, then you are coming from the emotion of fear: aggravation, annoyance, anger, rage, outrage, fury, wrath, hostility, ferocity, irritation, exasperation, disgust, revulsion, contempt, envy, jealousy, hurt, anguish, despair, gloom, grief, sorrow, misery, dismay, guilt, shame, regret, remorse, isolation, loneliness, rejection, defeat, insecurity, humiliation, insult, fright, horror, panic, anxiety, tenseness, apprehension, worry, dread or distress.

And just so you know… I did not make up this list; it was adapted from a psychology textbook titled, ***Emotions in Social Psychology*** by W. Gerrod Parrot.

Hormones and other chemicals produced in your body and brain by the feelings associated with the emotion of fear cause illness and distress. Hormones and other chemicals produced in the brain and body by the feelings associated with love cause health and well-being.

Create that ideal, fall in love with it; fall in love with life, with yourself and with your ability to be creative and you will live longer, be happier, healthier and more successful.

The following paragraphs may offend some readers and befuddle some others; but in order to provide some further elucidation about what level of desire I am talking about and why there is so much power in attaching that desire to your ideal, I must clarify what real desire and passion is all about.

In his seminal book, ***Think & Grow Rich***, Napoleon Hill writes about the transmutation of sexual energy into creative energy.

The kind of desire that carries real power is exactly like the passion you feel when you are in love or in lust with another person. This is the type of "tear your clothes off" feeling that you are aroused to when you desire to make love to your partner.

The truly empowered person is one who has learned, as Hill says, to transmute much of that sexual energy into creative energy and not squander it in vain physical pursuits.

We have, culturally, so many moralistic assumptions and beliefs about sexual energy that we prevent ourselves from fully understanding what it is and what it is capable of achieving when applied to a specific purpose.

Just as sexual energy can be used to awaken the power of Kundalini through Tantric ritual, so too can sexual energy empower you to become your most creative.

Sexual energy is also closely related to charisma and charisma attracts not only people, but wealth and power. So, learn to lust after your ideals. Fall in love. Be passionate. Imagine that your ideals are the sexiest thing in the world.

Quick Review:

Passion is the fire that lights your path and fuels your commitment as you walk into a future of your own creation.

Desire is the metaphysical equivalent of gravity. It draws to you the things, people and circumstances that you need to effectuate your ideals.

If the way you are feeling is not pleasant, then you are not acting in tune with your ideals. You are out of harmony. It is a sign that you need to change how you are being.

Direct Action Steps:

Spend ten minutes at the beginning of each day focusing your attention on your ideals. Imagine how it feels to have these as your reality.

Work yourself up into a fever of lust a few times a day about the things that you are in the process of creating in your life.

Whenever you find yourself feeling those feelings that are a subset of fear, stop, breathe and focus on your ideal and begin to feel loving.

"To me, there is only one form of human depravity -
the man without a purpose."

~ Ayn Rand

"In the works of man as in those of nature,
it is the intention which is chiefly worth studying."

~ Johann Wolfgang von Goethe

Chapter Three

Living On Purpose

When the father of my high school sweetheart asked me that not untypical question asked by fathers, "what is your intention regarding my daughter?", he had no idea how much he would, years later, transform my life, and the lives of many other people.

My reply was an honest and stammered "I don't know." What else could I answer? I had not actually thought about it. Of course, at that time in my life, it was my hormones and not my mind that governed my actions most of the time.

Many years later, another young lady asked me that same question. She was flirting. "What dear sir," she asked me, "are your intentions about me?" I knew the answer this time and answered her truthfully. "To bed you," I replied. It turned out to be the right answer. It matched her intention to a tee and I was pleased with the result. I trust she was too.

More importantly, it started me thinking. And soon, I was asking myself that life changing question everyday. "What is my intention in doing what I am doing right now?"

I have expanded that question over the years to include the various other aspects of my beingness.

What is my intention in thinking what I am thinking? What is my intention in feeling how I am feeling? What is my intention in believing that thing or idea?

If I do not have a clear answer and if what I am doing, thinking, feeling or believing at any given time does not actually serve me in some way, I stop. Then, I go about believing, thinking, feeling on purpose with specific intent.

What do I desire?

I want to be happy. Ok, so how does it serve me to be angry or frustrated? It doesn't, so there is no good reason to feel that way. I can choose to feel forgiveness instead of anger if someone does something not nice or inappropriate.

I want to be successful. Ok, so how does it serve me to waste hours of my life watching television? It doesn't. So I got rid of my television. There are only 1,440 minutes in each day. How many of them do you want to waste watching some mindless entertainment? For me, the answer is almost none.

I could go on and on about the ways my life has been transformed by asking myself that simple question, "what is my intention...?", but I think you already have the point.

As a result, my life is lived with a fair amount of intentionality. I still find myself occasionally doing things without any real purpose, but not all that often.

Now, when I am mentoring people, it is quite common for me to ask, "What is your intention in believing that?" (or thinking that, or saying that, or feeling that way). It usually startles people to be asked that in the same dramatic way I was startled by that father who was concerned about my intentions. Most people have just not ever thought about it.

When, for example, was the last time you asked yourself, "Why do I think that way? Does it serve me in some

46

way? Is there a purpose to thinking what I think? Or is it just random non-productive noise?"

Once you have created that ideal, or set of ideals, for yourself and your life, you will need to bring intentionality and purpose to your thoughts, beliefs, feelings and actions if you are ever to achieve that ideal.

The four principle elements of conscious creation are: thought, desire, belief and intent. Self-mastery is attained when one establishes conscious control of all four elements.

Creating a life of abundant happiness and success is all about bringing congruity to your self and the way that you go about being in the world. Form your ideals in your imagination. Visualize them in their completeness. Be passionate about them. Desire their materialization. Affirm their reality to build your belief. Be grateful for their existence. Then act as if they were already existent in the material as well as in the imaginal by doing those things that support them.

In other words, be, do and have in agreement, in accord, with your ideals and you will produce or create their manifestation. Be congruous. Act harmoniously. Have accordance with your ideals. You will be living your life 'on purpose'. Success will naturally result.

Sadly, most people live lives happenstancially, with only rare and fleeting moments of clarity of purpose. The good news is that anyone can start today to live a life of meaning and purpose by bringing intentionality to their lives.

It is often said that the purpose of life is to live a life of purpose. Unfortunately, so many people stumble around vainly attempting to figure out some grand purpose for their life, not knowing that if they only brought intentionality to each present moment, their life would be filled with both purpose and meaning.

In conversation with one of the people I coached a few months ago, she said to me, "I did not intend for my life to turn out this way?" It was the perfect opening for me. "How did you intend for it to turn out?" I asked. "I don't know, but not like this," she answered. "So, if you had no clear intent, then how can you possibly expect anything except some random unplanned result?" was my next question.

These are hard questions to be sure, but the truth is that if you are not living each day of your life on purpose, then how can you possibly expect it to turn out anyway except accidentally.

It is ok for a child to say, "I didn't do it on purpose," in response to some accidental event; but it is not acceptable for any adult human being to pretend that they are not responsible for the things that happen in their life.

The cold hard truth is that if your life is not living up to your expectations, it is because you have made some inappropriate choices that have resulted in you having the results you have. If you would rather have your things show up in your life by choice rather than by chance, then start asking yourself as often as possible the following questions. What is my intention in doing what I am about to do? Is there a purpose to what I am thinking, how I am feeling, what I am doing? What do I expect to get out of it? What result will this action produce? Why am I doing this thing?

Why? is always the best question. It is not what; not who; not where; not when; not even how; but the question "why?" that is the best source of both wisdom and power. As soon as you begin to ask yourself why, you begin to accumulate both power and wisdom.

Yes, you can learn a lot by asking what, who, where, when and how; but in asking why, you get to the heart of the matter. For example, what you think is critically important; BUT **why you think what you think is even more crucial**; AND, knowing why you think what you think will give you enormous insight into who you are and how you are creating what you have in life.

Why do you think what you think? What is your intent? Why do you believe in what you believe? Do you have any intent in believing in that? Why do you feel the way you feel? To what end? Why do you do what you do? Why do you have what you have? The answers may provide insight; but it is the asking of the question that is the source of any wisdom gained. The answers may show potential; but it is the asking of the question that demonstrates your willingness to express your personal power. The question really comes down to... what exactly are your intentions?

It is really quite simple. Thoughts, thought thoughtlessly; beliefs, believed in without critical examination; emotions allowed in reaction; things done without a clear and purposeful intent will produce unintended results. When you are being and acting without intentionality, you are simply a creature of event and circumstance. When you bring intentionality to all that you are and all that you do, you become a causal agent and can consciously create the events and circumstances that will provide the ease and abundance you desire.

Without intention, the way things unfold in your life appear to be confusing and even, perhaps, chaotic. When your intention is applied, the way things unfold in the universe appear to be harmonious and in sync with your own ideals and expectations. It is your intentionality that brings a harmony of thought, word and deed and it is this harmony that puts you into the flow of things.

Your intent is the expression of your will. Your will is your personal power. If you allow yourself to hold any thoughts or beliefs or emotions or allow yourself to perform any actions without a very specific intention as the primary motivation, then you are not claiming your power and not expressing your will. And you are not living on purpose.

When your predominant and repetitive thought patterns are intentionally chosen, when your core beliefs are intentionally and consciously chosen, when your primary emotions or prevailing attitudes are consciously and intentionally chosen, when what you do and what you enact is done on purpose and with purpose, with intentionality, you are powerful indeed.

So pay attention to your intentions.

What are your predominant thought patterns? Why do you choose to think those repetitive thoughts? Why do you choose to think anything you think? To what end? Does it serve you in any way to think what you actually think? Is there any clear intent behind most of your thoughts or is this stream of consciousness that is constantly running through your mind just random noise?

If you are honest with yourself, you will see, like most people who indulge in this self-reflection, that 95% of what goes on in your mind has not been consciously chosen to serve some defined end or goal and, in all likelihood, does not actually serve you in any discernable way.

Here is the good news. You can actually train your mind to think mostly those thoughts that do serve you in living your ideals and achieving your goals. Sure, it takes some discipline at first to develop new habitual ways of thinking, but the rewards for being in control of your own mind are enormous. And as you practice this mental control over what goes on in your mind, it gets easier and easier.

A person who thinks on purpose, who chooses his or her thoughts intentionally, who stops thinking those thoughts that serve no useful purpose, who focuses his thoughts on his ideals and goals, ends up being not only successful, but happier and more fulfilled.

Learning to think for yourself makes you very powerful. You become capable of consciously creating the life you envision and desire for yourself. It is more than worth the effort.

One of the most important realizations that anyone can come to is that thoughts create reality. **Your thoughts create your reality.** It is not just that the way you think that determines how you interpret the world; the way you think also determines how you behave and thus create results.

Thoughts actually become things. This is not new news. It's not some ethereal theory. It's not a fanciful philosophy without any direct application to your day-to-day life.

It is the single most important piece of knowledge possessed by humanity. It is the primary cause behind your success or failure in life.

What was once known only to metaphysicists is now also known by physicists. It is a scientific fact. Thought creates.

I am not just referring to the kind of creative thought that brings about art or technology. All thought creates all the time. Your every single thought is creating your reality in every moment.

I'll say it again for emphasis... your thoughts create your reality. Bluntly, if your reality sucks, it is because your thinking sucks.

The great good news is that if you desire to change your reality, it is as simple as changing your thinking. In order to improve your life, you only need to improve your thinking.

Simple? Well, there are a couple of impediments. These are what hold most people back from profound change or improvements. They act in the same way that an electronic invisible fence serves to keep a dog from roaming free.

First, you are accustomed to (or addicted to) thinking a certain way. You have been trained to think a certain way. Most people are too lazy or too scared to think original or intentional thoughts. Most people actually do not even pay any attention to what they are thinking. They don't know what they are thinking or why they are thinking what they think. Do you?

Second, you exist within a consensual societal reality picture, a collective consciousness, a meta-meme, that serves to limit your ability to have original thoughts. Most people blindly accept the norms of their cultural conditioning; things are the way they are... that is reality. They ignore the fact that it is those who have challenged the normal thinking patterns, those who have thought outside the box, that have brought about the advances in human society or that have created their own extraordinary and successful lives.

So, in order to transform your thinking, and thus, your reality, you must exercise a purposeful discipline. You must learn how to think on purpose. You must resist your tendency to revert to old ingrained habitual thinking. You must decide to opt out of the mass-mind and act as an individual, intentionally choosing what, how and why you think what you think.

First, figure out exactly what you are thinking; what are your predominant repetitive thought patterns. Pay attention to your thoughts. Where do they come from? Why do you think that thought? What does it create in your life?

Second, decide (choose) to think those specific thoughts that will serve to create the reality you desire to see manifest in your life.

Every artifact, every tool, everything ever designed or created by human beings for their own need, comfort, luxury, amusement or advancement began as an idea, a concept... a thought.

All wealth had its origins in thought. It is thought that creates. Everything that human beings have created is a

product of mind. Wealth is created; it is the effect; thought is the cause.

A penny for your thoughts? How about a billion pennies instead for just one thought? No matter how you define wealth, your attainment of this wealth will depend upon the quality and consistency of your thinking combined with the clear and firm desire to realize what you idealize.

It is patently obvious that, since your mind is the cause and what you have is the effect, the place to work on your wealth is in your own mind.

Those who achieve and keep great wealth have learned to control the quality and consistency of their thoughts, their attitudes and their desires. They have learned to think 'on purpose' instead of accidentally.

If you can, despite all distractions and obstacles, keep your mind focused upon what you idealize and desire, you will move steadily toward creating or realizing your ideal/thought.

Most people do not do this. They allow conditions and circumstances to determine how they think, how they feel and what they end up with. Their allowingness of that which is outside of themselves to control their mind and their results turns them into victims.

Those, who, through the use of their will, use that which is inside themselves, that is... their own mind, their consciousness, their idealizations, their thoughts, their desires, their passions and their beliefs to control who they are and what they create, end up as victors in the game of life.

In other words, if you want to have more out of life, you must first become more. Since it is in your nature to want more, the only way you can find any kind of personal fulfillment is to become more.

It does not matter what it is that you want more of; the only way to get it is to become more. You become more by taking control of your self… your mind, your passions, your beliefs, then your words and deeds and thus… your results or what you end up having.

There is a simple, yet profound, formula for creating success… be > do > have. Or, I as prefer to express it… become > enact > attain.

If a hundred people are given exactly the same opportunity and the same resources to exploit that opportunity and the same playing field to take advantage of that opportunity, and 10 people excel at that opportunity and 10 fail (80% are average or mediocre), where is the difference?

The answer is that since the only variable in the equation is within each of the people, it is the mind, mental attitude or will-ing-ness to grow and become more that determines those who win and those who lose (and those in the majority, who will, for comfort sake, remain average).

Losers will, of course, blame it on anything else and refuse to accept responsibility for being at cause. Winners will have chosen to become and do what was necessary to take advantage of the opportunity. They have accepted that they, themselves, are at cause and are grateful for the opportunity to prove that they can succeed, to prove that they are masters of their own destiny, not victims of fate and fortune.

So ask yourself, what are you thinking? A penny's worth?? A million$ worth?? Just exactly what are you thinking and why? What is your intention in thinking what you are thinking? Want more out of life? Take control of yourself. Think on purpose, not by accident. Live your life by design and not by default.

Most people never achieve the levels of success and happiness they aspire to. And these 90% of people willfully ignore the fact that 90% of the time, 90% of their thoughts are creating results they do not intend or desire.

Always, according to these people, it is the outside conditions and circumstances that are to blame for their lack of hoped for results. They steadfastly refuse to closely examine their own thought processes and steadfastly refuse to accept responsibility for what and how they think.

I'll tell you this... if you really, really desire to create for yourself the ideals of wealth, health and happiness you hold, you will have to learn to think on purpose. A hammer is a tool. A chisel is a tool. Anyone can use them to chip away at concrete. Michelangelo used them to create the statue of David (and more). The mind is a tool. Many use it to chip away at life. A few use it to create their ideals, the life of their dreams. Your mind is your own. It is a tool. How you use it is up to you.

We can all see the stupidity of someone wanting to be healthy and fit but spending their evenings channel surfing in front of the boob tube eating junk food. It is the same as wanting to be wealthy while spending most of the time thinking random non-productive thoughts.

Physical exercise produces results. So does mental exercise. Living on a diet of junk food will prevent or destroy your health. Living on a diet of mental junk will prevent or destroy your wealth. Simple thing to understand; yet most folks live on mental junk. They watch mindless drivel on TV. They allow societal programming to dominate their thought processes. They don't examine what they are thinking. They don't make the effort to think on purpose. They don't flex their mental muscles.

Can you think and grow rich? You bet. That is how all riches are created. Most, however, are more habituated to the "think and grow poor" way of life. Opt out of the mass mindset. Start thinking creatively. Start thinking wealthy thoughts.

The laws of the universe are immutable. One such law is that thought creates. Like gravity, it works all the time, not just when you want it to. Your every thought is creative. Scattered thoughts create scattered results and that sometimes confuses people and leads them to believe that thought is not always creative. 15 minutes per day of positive, focused, purposeful thought cannot completely override 23 hours and 45 minutes of unfocused, negative and accidental thought.

If your results are mixed, it is because the quality of your thoughts is mixed.

You can deny but not escape that plain and simple truth.

Do you want to create intended and desired results? Get control of your thoughts. Do you yearn to be wealthy? Think your way to riches. Think on purpose. Get the wealth consciousness. Adopt a prosperity paradigm. Start living each moment on purpose. Be intentional.

Quick Review:

If what you are thinking, believing and feeling is not done with a conscious, intentional purpose, it is likely that your life will unfold accidentally. In other words, your choice is to create a life by design or by default.

Always ask yourself why. Why am I thinking this way? Why do I believe that? Why am I feeling this way? You are able to choose how and what to think. You are able to choose what to believe. You are able to choose how to feel. When you bring intentionality to those choices, your life takes on meaning and purpose and you come into your power to be a consciously creative being.

Direct Action Steps:

Make a list of the things you did yesterday, hour by hour, and then ask yourself which of those activities were directly contributory to your stated ideals.

Resolve to act intentionally and to live on purpose.

Develop the habit of asking yourself what your intention is in doing what you are doing. Always ask why.

Maya

Illusion works impenetrable,
Weaving webs innumerable,
Her gay pictures never fail,
Crowds each other, veil on veil,
Charmer who will be believed,
By man who thirsts to be deceived.

~ Ralph Waldo Emerson

"Reality is merely an illusion,
albeit a very persistent one."
~ Albert Einstein

Chapter Four

Seeing Beyond The Veil

Belief is a critical element of your ability to create success for yourself. As James Allen, the author of "As A Man Thinketh" reminds us, "The outer conditions of a person's life will always be found to reflect their inner beliefs."

You must learn to believe that your firmly held ideal is at least as real as (or even more real than) the current events and circumstances of your life (the evidence of your senses); and more fully true than any apparent limitation, impediment or obstacle that may stand between you and the fulfillment of your ideal.

Because we live in a temporal world and there is a delay between cause and effect, the things that you have in your life right now are a result of how you used to be and what you have done in the past. So, if you today transform the way you are (alter your predominant thought patterns and habitual way of feeling) and change the way you behave (the things you habitually do), your results will, over time, change. That is an almost inevitable conclusion.

It is almost inevitable, but not necessarily so. The caveat is that if you continue to expect things to remain the same, they most likely will, despite any personal changes you decide to make.

Your expectations are determined by your beliefs. If you believe that the evidence of your senses comprises the whole of your reality, then you will expect that things will continue to evolve as they have. You will expect that the future will be a continuation of the past. In other words, if you choose to believe that the world you perceive is real and your ideal is still only an imaginal concept, then you will have created an expectation that things will unfold as they historically have done.

I'll let you in on a little secret... life delivers pretty much what you expect it will. If you want to have success in life, you must train yourself to expect success.

The English word "expect" is actually a contraction of 2 Latin roots "ex" and "spect" and its literal meaning is "to out-picture". When you look at the world, you do not perceive what is actually there, you see what your mind expects to see. What does your mind expect to see? What it has been trained to see.

The world, as you see and experience it, is just your personal internal reality picture out-pictured or expected. Your reality is first pre-conceived or visualized inside your mind. Your mind then projects that internal image onto the world and that internal picture thus becomes your external reality.

What you have in life is based on your expectations. Your expectations are governed by your paradigms. And, a paradigm is a set of experiences, beliefs, values and assumptions that affect the way an individual perceives reality and responds to that perception.

Your expectations are built upon your beliefs... what you believe you could have, or what you believe you should have, or what you believe you deserve to have. Where did you get those beliefs about your possibilities, potentials, limitations and deservingness?

Mostly, you inherit them. You just take them on, assume them, without examining them for veracity or usefulness.

If you ask most people "Why do you believe such and such?" Most will answer, "Because it is true." And since 'being right' is one of the ways we validate who we are, we will stubbornly argue that our beliefs are real and true even when we have not examined them ourselves to see if there is, in fact, any validity or value in a particular belief.

No matter what rationalizations or intellectual convolutions are brought to bear in an attempt to prove how or why something is true, in the end it is really no different than the childish refrain, "Why?" — " Because."

Only when you are able to honestly answer, "I believe in such and such because it serves me to believe in such and such," will you be in control of your destiny and success.

Take a moment and check in with your self to ask these simple questions:

- Do you believe it is possible for you to achieve a large degree of success?
- Do you believe that you deserve to have a large degree of success?
- Do you believe that the world is set up to support your success?
- Do you believe that your success will come easily and naturally?
- Do you believe that success is your birthright or something to be earned?

Now ask yourself:

- Why do I hold those beliefs? How did I come by them?
- Do those beliefs serve me in any way? How?

- What personal expectations have come out of those beliefs?

From the moment we arrive in this world, we are trained to expect certain things or trained to expect for things to be a certain way. Our culture, our personal experiences, our parents, our education, our peers all serve to train us to have certain expectations in life. And, for the most part, these expectations are self-fulfilling prophecies.

We expect something; it shows up; we then say, "see, it was true." We forget the fact that it is only true because we first believed it to be true and then expected it to be true. We ignore the fact that if we held different beliefs and expectations in the first place, then the truth would be different.

Now you might say in response to the above, "I did not expect my life to turn out this way or I did not expect for the world to be this way, it just is."

To which I will reply, "What exactly were you expecting?" I am willing to bet that you have pretty much the results that you were expecting to have; and that if you critically and honestly examine your core beliefs, you will understand why you were expecting exactly what you have.

If you desire to have a meaningful and measurable amount of success in life, you are going to have to train your mind to expect success; not hope for; not wish for; but fully expect success.

To do that training, you are going to need to provide new information to your mind so that it can be convinced to take on different beliefs. You will need to undertake a program to consciously brainwash yourself. Opt out of the culture of mediocrity and opt into the culture of success. Read success literature. Hang around successful people. Affirm your right to success.

Do the things that have been proven to work. Stop doing the things that have been proven, by your own experience, to not work. Break your addiction to mediocrity or failure. Get addicted to success.

Recently, while hiking up an escarpment with an old karma mate, he asked me, "If you could only say one thing, what would be the most important understanding you'd like to impart?"

My answer was immediate, "Everything exists entirely in your imagination."

I have already introduced you to this idea in Chapter One, but since you, like me, were probably told several times in your childhood, "it's only in your imagination", you are probably stuck into thinking that the things of the imagination are not really real; so, allow to me to explain how even the so-called real world exists **entirely** in your imagination.

One of my teachers, who was attempting to teach me discernment, told me, "do not believe anything unless you see it with your own eyes". At a certain level, there may be some value in that, but it is, overall, a poor piece of advice that ignores the true nature of reality.

Your eyes do not, in fact, see anything.

Just like a camera lens does not actually see, but only focuses light waves, your eyes only focus light waves onto your optic nerve. This stimulation of your optic nerve by electromagnetic energy creates a virtual lightening storm of neural activity in your brain. Your mind then interprets this sparking pattern of neural activity as the image perceived. The image is created in your imagination. It is your mind that sees, not your eyes. What you actually see is the image that exists in and is created by your imagination.

Modern physics has shown us that everything in the universe, at its most fundamental or true level, is simply and elegantly comprised of various frequencies of vibrating energy. A myriad of vibrations are constantly interacting with each other to create interference patterns that constitute the sub-atomic particles. Sub-atomic particles congregate to form atoms, then molecules, then complex structures like a rock or a tree or a human body.

When light (electromagnetic energy) bounces off these complex interference patterns and gets focused through your eye lens onto your optic nerve, which in turn stimulates that electrochemical storm of neural activity in your brain, your mind creates the image of the rock.

The rock you see exists in your imagination. Your experience of rock is entirely subjective and internal. The external reality is, in truth, the interference pattern created by the interacting vibrations. It is that wondrous aspect of mind called imagination that creates your image of, your perception of and your experience of that thing called rock.

At the deepest and most fundamental level of reality, there is no boundary between you and your world. You are not separate from universe and universe is not separate from you. There is only yoUniverse.

You are constantly creating your experience by the choices you make. In fact, the choices you make

determine who you are as well as what you have as an experience.

There is no objective reality. The observer and the observed are one and the same essence. It is impossible for the observer to have anything except a subjective experience because he cannot step outside of the system he exists within. And, since the very act of existing within and observing the system itself has an effect on what is observed, you are constantly in the process of creating your reality.

The words on this page have no meaning until you give them meaning. The events and circumstances of your life have no value until you impart a value to them.

The ideals you construct in your imagination are as real as anything else that exists.

When you allow that so called objective and external world of event and circumstance to determine your reality picture, you are allowing the illusionary and transitory to distract you from the greater truth that all things exist only in your imagination.

Moreover, everything you perceive is in the past. That is correct. Nothing you observe in the external world exists in this present moment. It is all something that happened in the past. Stand outside on a cloudless night and observe the star filled sky. Pick out any star; say the middle star in Orion's belt, Alnilam.

Is it really there? There is no way you can be sure of that. It is more than 1300 light years away. It could have ceased to exist a thousand years ago and yet, you still perceive it to be there.

Closer to home, our own star, Sol, the sun that lights your life, could have ceased to exist 5 minutes ago and you would not be aware of that yet because the radiation emitted by the sun takes almost nine minutes to reach your eyes. It looks like it is still there (and I sure hope it is), but can you say for sure that it is? Nope. The only thing you can say for sure is that the image of it still exists in your imagination.

And that is true of everything you perceive. It is all in the past and it is all the result of past causes. None of it exists in your actual present moment.

The only things that really exist in this present moment are the images you hold in your imagination. So how could you possibly allow yourself to believe that current events and circumstances are more real than the ideal you create in your imagination?

Believe in your self. You are real. Believe in your dreams, your ideals, your goals. They are real. Believe in what inspires you. That is real.

Everything else is just a passing illusion.

Quick Review:

You are constantly creating your reality picture by your choices. Freedom and power comes from asking yourself what do you believe and why do you believe it?

Life delivers what you expect it to produce.

Everything you perceive has already happened. It is in the past. Only that which you imagine exists in this present moment.

Direct Action Steps:

Ask yourself what you would like to believe about yourself.

Then ask what you can do today to make that belief be more true.

Then do it.

"Gratitude unlocks the fullness of life. It turns what we have into enough, and more. It turns denial into acceptance, chaos to order, confusion to clarity. It can turn a meal into a feast, a house into a home, a stranger into a friend. Gratitude makes sense of our past, brings peace for today, and creates a vision for tomorrow."

~ Melody Beattie

"The most fortunate are those who have a wonderful capacity to appreciate again and again, freshly and naively, the basic goods of life, with awe, pleasure, wonder, and even ecstasy."
~ Abraham Maslow

Chapter Five

Living in Grace

If you were to take a piece of paper and a pen and start now to write down a list of all the blessings that you have in your life, it would occupy you for the remainder of the days you have available to you.

The hand that grasps the pen, the mind that catalogues the blessings, the will that makes the choices, the lungs that breathe each breath, the heart that pumps your blood to your brain, the eyes that enable you to see the words, the ability to read and write, the sunshine that lights the page, the opportunity to choose the attitude of gratitude are just a few quick examples of the endless list of things that you have to appreciate.

Your life is filled with blessings. Most of these you take for granted, not even thinking about them. This devalues, not only the things themselves, but also you, yourself.

Learning to honor all things as being valuable, even sacred, and understand how blessed you are to have the opportunity to play this game called Life on Planet Earth increases the value of you, your life and opens you up to receive even more abundance and blessings.

Gratefulness brings a great fullness to life. **The choice to adopt and hold a moment-by-moment attitude of gratitude is the choice that differentiates those who suffer the slings and arrows of misfortune and those who are blessed with a joyous and abundant life.**

Yes, that is correct. It is not the actual events and circumstances that occur during one's journey through life that determine whether or not a person is happy and prosperous; it is the conscious and willful choice to be grateful for all the bounty that life has to offer AND to be grateful for the opportunity to participate in and contribute to the experience of life, which enables and empowers any individual, regardless of circumstance, to have a fulfilling and rewarding life.

Like everything else on the path to mastery, gratitude is a choice. You can choose to wait for some meaningfully pleasant situation to arise and then feel gratitude in response, or you can choose to be grateful at all times, in all circumstances, and watch as the world conspires to assist you in your path.

If you are grateful for what you already have, the world will conspire to give you more to be grateful for. If you are resentful of what you already have, the world will conspire to give you more to resent.

Moreover, the true master learns to be grateful, in advance, for the things that are idealized and desired. Why? Because, being grateful in advance for some attainment or accomplishment does two very important things: first, it tricks your subconscious into believing that the goal is certain and second, it convinces other people, with whom you must interact to achieve your desires, that you know what you are about, that you are a winner.

When your subconscious is convinced that the goal is certain, it will provide the ways and means of fulfilling or achieving that goal. Since your subconscious is connected to the great collective subconscious of humanity, it also informs this 'morphic field' of your profound intent and the result is that the people, resources and conditions for fulfillment will show up in your life. All this will happen because you chose to be grateful in advance of the havingness. The act of being grateful in advance is proof of your faith and belief in the actuality, eventuality and realness of the manifestation of your desired ideal.

And when other people are convinced that you are convinced of the realness of your goals because of your demonstrative gratitude for their reality, they will rally around you and provide both physical and metaphysical support for you and your goals.

The benefits of the physical support (the investment of time, effort and money) to contribute to you and your goals are obvious. What may not be obvious, to those unfamiliar with the laws of the universe, is that the metaphysical support is even more crucial. The added belief of others in you and your goals brings an 'aura' of success about you that creates, in turn, even more support for you.

The knowledge that all things, existent and potential, are, at their pure essence, a myriad of interlocking and interwoven vibrations of pure energy and that the emanations of your consciousness (and the emanations of the other individual consciousnesses of the people who associate with you) interfere with and interact with pre-existing vibrations to create new patterns that result in the manifestation of actualities is what denotes wisdom and mastery.

If other people are convinced that you are a successful person, their energetic output (thought and belief) will serve to enhance your own power to enact the Law of Attraction to produce the results you desire.

All this, and more, happens when you choose to hold and to express gratefulness for what you have and what you claim or expect to have as you journey through life.

Begin each day with an expression of your gratitude for all the blessings that life has bestowed upon you and your day will be filled with even more and greater blessings.

The choice is yours. Every breath you breathe can be an expression of gratitude. Existing in a state of gratefulness is very alike existing in a state of grace. Your blessings multiply constantly.

Being grateful denotes your knowledge of, and application of, one of the most important aspects of creation… **who you are and how you are produces what you have.**

And gratitude, of course, makes what you have all that much more enjoyable.

Most people sleepwalk through life, unaware of the majesty of this universe we live in and participate in creating, unappreciative of their own opportunity to become conscious creators and contributors.

Those who are fully awake live in a constant state of wonder and appreciation that in some moments even escalates from wonder to joy and from appreciation to that state of profound gratitude for the gifts of life and self-awareness that is called bliss.

There exists a magical power in the feeling of gratitude.

Yes, a magical power.

However, before I talk about the magic of gratitude, I want to talk about its opposite. Not the lack of gratitude, not even ingratitude; but resentfulness.

Powerful emotions attached to specific repetitive thoughts make things manifest. Intentional thought combined with heartfelt desire is how masters and winners create the circumstances and events of their lives. This powerful knowledge is one of the most crucial things a person who desires to be a creator instead of a mere creature needs to know and integrate into their life.

There is a dark side. Just as what you love/desire can come true, so too, as even the bible reminds us... that what you fear shall come to pass. You can easily witness the power of fear making things happen in many people's lives. A victim's attitude often creates events that cause that person to say, "see, I told you so." They don't, of course, know that it was their very own fear that attracted the bad thing into their life. It is the proverbial self-fulfilling prophecy.

It works the same with gratitude and resentfulness. When you walk around with the attitude of gratitude, life does not just seem better because of your psychological take on life, it actually is better because of the magic creative power of intentionally combining positive thought and positive emotion.

However, if you adopt the attitude of resentfulness, things don't just seem bad... bad things actually do happen more often than they would otherwise. Resentfulness is insidious. Once you start to resent the circumstances and conditions of your life, you begin attracting more things into your life that you will not welcome UNTIL AND UNLESS you change your attitude.

Some molehill appears on your path and your resentfulness makes it into a mountain blocking your way forward. The next thing you know, a real mountain shows up. Why? Because you attracted it by your way of being. And now it is harder to be grateful instead of resentful.

That is why masters at the art of living see obstacles as an opportunity to learn, to grow, to become more powerful; and, winners see obstacles as proof that they are traveling the high road. They know that the flat, wide, easy road is the path of mediocrity. It is wide, flat and easy because it is well traveled by the majority, those who do not aspire or dare to achieve great things, or to challenge life and themselves to deliver more than the norm.

Losers resent winners. You see it all the time. Even the average person delights in the often public trials and tribulations of the high achievers. These people stubbornly refuse to comprehend that it is their own resentfulness that actually makes them losers with much in their own lives to resent. They also don't understand that the winner is grateful not just because things are going right, but because it is the initial choice to feel a sense of gratitude that makes things go right in the first place.

Resentfulness is insidious. You may not even be aware that you harbor an unconscious resentfulness of successful people. But pay close attention! If you even once have thought that such and such a person does not deserve the success they have accomplished, there is an element of resentfulness in your heart. This resentment will handicap you from achieving your own success.

Learn instead to celebrate the successes of everyone. After all, you would want others to celebrate your own success. It is the simple application of the Golden Rule... Do unto others as you would have them do unto you. Learn to celebrate other people's success. Extend your empathy when they stumble.

If you want to be a winner, start being grateful; start existing in a constant state of thanksgiving. Start celebrating your own life and your own blessings right now. You don't need some annual celebration of some romanticized historical event to feel grateful and give thanks. As long as you are still breathing, you have much to be thankful for.

Begin right now. Make a list of all the things that you have to be grateful for having already received. Let me start you off with some basics you may not think of on your own.

- You can read. One out of every five adults alive today is illiterate and cannot read this sentence.
- You can afford to buy this book. About half the population on this planet lives on less than $2 per day and cannot adequately afford to pay for the basic essentials of life, let alone some book about improving the quality of their life.
- You have the opportunity right now to create an abundant, fulfilling and contributory life. Most people are unaware of how to go about doing that. Remember this: if you are reading this, you should know that you are better off than the overwhelming majority of other people on this planet.

There are so many things to be grateful for that you could spend all day every day simply listing them; yet so many instead spend so much time cataloging their various perceived misfortunes. Complain, complain, complain is the common refrain.

Complaining about the trials and tribulations of life seems to be the norm rather than celebrating the joys and wonders that are present in everyone's life, no matter what circumstances they may encounter in any given moment.

This focus of attention on what is not considered the ideal not only creates an attitude that prevents the enjoyment of the blessings you do have, but also contributes to ensuring that you will continue to create more frustration and disappointment.

When you make the conscious choice to begin expressing your continuous gratitude, you will find that the quality of your life improves dramatically and that the success you desire is attracted into your life.

You have, right now, and always, the chance to appreciate and to honor all you have been given. You have, right now, and always, the chance to enjoy the pleasures of walking around on planet earth. You have, right now, and always, the chance to make a meaningful difference in the lives of other people.

Give thanks. You'll end up with plenty to be grateful for.

To be grateful for something means to appreciate its value. The word appreciate has two meanings. I'll let Merriam Webster's dictionary explain…

1 a: to grasp the nature, worth, quality, or significance of **b:** to value or admire highly **c:** to judge with heightened perception or understanding : be fully aware of   d: to recognize with gratitude **2**: to increase the value of

An investment that appreciates over time becomes more valuable. Anything that you have that you appreciate becomes more valuable. If you really appreciate what you already have and what you are enabled to idealize and realize, then your life will become filled with even more valuables to appreciate.

You can express your gratitude to some deity; you can express your gratitude to the universe; you can express your gratitude to thin air. It matters not to whom or to what you express your gratitude; it only matters that you FEEL grateful. It is the emotional energy that creates the power.

The energetic strength of your consciously chosen emotional output can transform your life from frustration to fulfillment, from paucity to prosperity, from lack to abundance, from failure to success.

Change your overall attitude and predominant feelings from fear into love, from resentment into gratitude, from misery to joy and you will find yourself empowered to create a life of success almost as if by magic. Fear is a choice of attitude. Love is a choice. Resentment is a choice. Gratitude is a choice. Misery is a choice. Joy is a choice. Knowing that, what do you choose?

The word scared can be transformed into the word sacred simply by moving the letter 'c'. Similarly, your life can be transformed simply by moving your seeing (perspective) of life and its many blessings.

The magic power of gratitude is this: the more you are and feel grateful for what you already have, the more that you will have to be grateful for. Do you want more? Learn to be more grateful.

Quick Review:

The attitude of gratitude makes life more enjoyable and brings ever more things to be grateful for having. It is an endless upward spiral.

Gratitude has a magic power that convinces your subconscious, other people and the universe that you recognize your own value and the value of the many blessings you already have and thus, you deserve to have even more to appreciate.

Direct Action Steps:

Each day, before getting out of bed, spend ten minutes expressing your gratitude for all the blessings you have in your life. Mentally list a few of these many things that you enjoy having and your day will unfold as if you were especially blessed.

Each night, before going to sleep, spend ten minutes expressing your gratitude for the things that you are in the process of creating. If you fall asleep while doing this, it is even better, because your subconscious mind, that does not sleep, will be working to process this information and will supply you with the ideas you need to make your dreams come true.

"It is not by prayer and humility that you cause things to go as you wish, but by acquiring a knowledge of natural laws"

~ Bertrand Russell

"Every person has free choice. Free to obey or disobey the Natural Laws. Your choice determines the consequences. Nobody ever did, or ever will, escape the consequences of his choices."

~ Alfred Montapert

Chapter Six

Playing By The Rules

Ah, the rules…

How can you play to win if you do not know the rules of the game?

Creating success means winning, according to your own definition of what it means to win at the game of life. In other words, winning means to create and live a successful life according to your own ideals and definitions.

If you want to win, you will need to learn to play by the rules.

Of course, there are rules. There are rules that govern almost everything. There are rules that determine the behavior of raindrops falling and planets orbiting stars. There are rules that determine the behavior of electrons and the behavior of black holes. There are rules that govern why an apple falls to the ground and how matter can be converted to energy.

And, there are certain fundamental rules that apply to the essential existence of the universe. There is a reason that all things happen the way they happen.

All science (the search for the why and the how that things happen they way they do) is based on the fundamental assumption that there is a cause behind everything, an identifiable process (or series of processes) that causes the world to be the way it is and to behave the way it does.

Why ask why? Why ask how? We assume that there exists an answer. When something happens, we assume (take for granted) that something caused it. Reason says that there must be a reason. It is our nature to ask questions (why and how), so we expect there to always be an answer, even if it is difficult to discover.

When some fundamental process that answers a profound question is discovered and identified, it is called a Basic Scientific Principle or a Natural Law. Question: Why does the apple fall to the ground? Answer: Gravity, which along with the Weak Nuclear Force, the Strong Nuclear Force and Electromagnetism is one of the four fundamental forces that enable the existence of the universe.

Metaphysics understands that every physical thing or condition has some metaphysical cause. I am using the word metaphysical here as that "which is beyond the physical". Since these Principles or Laws are beyond the physical, they can be called Metaphysical Laws.

These Laws or rules determine how the physical world comes into being and behaves. It is common also for people to equate metaphysical with spiritual, so these Laws are also often called Spiritual Laws by those folks who like that terminology.

Many people say that Cause and Effect is a Natural Law, but since it is the basic assumption that determines the whole scientific approach, it must be termed a meta-law: the rule that determines how all other rules are defined.

This basic assumption that all things happen because of some basic cause (or causes) says that some fundamental force is always responsible for something else that is happening eventually leads to the inescapable conclusion that there is a prime cause. It can't be "turtles all the way down". It is one thing to say that The Big Bang was the responsible cause of the entire unfolding universe; but what caused this Big Bang?

Prime Cause is, of course, still a mystery to us, so the best we can do is to identify certain universal principles or Natural Laws and use them to understand how the world works and also to create what we desire to have.

You don't need to know Prime Cause to start a fire to cook a meal to alleviate your hunger. You just have to know how to start a fire. Once upon a time, humans did not know how to start a fire. Now we do. And we know a bunch of other important things as well. But, as I have said before, knowing something is not enough to produce the effects we desire. You can know how to start a fire, but if you don't actually do it, you still can't cook that meal.

If success is an effect, then there must be a cause. So, even if it appears that someone's success happened by accident or luck, logic tells us that there must have been a cause or set of causes.

Even accidents don't happen accidentally. There is always a cause. When an airplane crashes, the FAA does not say, "oh it was an accident" and let it go at that. They look for the cause and determine how to fix things so that it does not happen again. Or, if a scientist accidentally discovers a new chemical compound, he does not say to himself, "oh, it was an accident" and not attempt to reproduce the process. He looks for the causal agents.

Strangely, many people live their lives as if everything were either an accident or as if it were all the responsibility of this mysterious Prime Cause. Why am I suffering? It is God's will. It is fate. It is just the way things are. They allow themselves to be mere creatures of event and circumstance. They think that other successful people are just lucky or blessed for some unknown reason.

Thankfully, there are people who look for why things happen and then, use that knowledge to make things happen. These people are creators of event and circumstance. Without them, we still would not be able to light that fire to cook our meals or build that orbiting space station or consciously create any idealized and desired effect, like success.

Hungry? Want to cook some food? Learn how to light a fire. Then light it. Let hunger be your motivation, not your condition.

Want success? Learn how to create success, then, go about doing what is necessary. To want can mean "to lack"; to want can mean "to desire". Lack is a condition. Desire is a motivation. Let your wanting be your motivation, not your condition.

Everyone has the choice to be a creature of event and circumstance or to become a creator of event and circumstance. In other words, you can become a consciously causal agent and the effects that are the events and circumstances of your life can be molded by your desires. How? By learning what the Natural Laws (the rules of the game) are and learning how to apply them to make things happen.

The Meta-Law :: The Law of Cause and Effect: There is a cause behind every effect.

There is a reason why things are the way they are. Nothing exists in isolation. In other words, there is always an explanation or understanding of how things came to be and are the way they are, of why things happen the way that they do happen.

In today's world, believing that things happen for no reason, or without a cause, or because of luck is accepted as superstition. Yet strangely enough, many people somehow think that their life is the way it is because of luck or fate. A person who can think rationally knows that this is superstitious nonsense. Any effects you have in your life are the result of certain identifiable causes.

We know that viruses or bacteria are the cause behind certain infections. We don't blame them on luck or the gods, like people in the Middle Ages blamed The Black Plaque as being God's wrath and some people today blame AIDS on God's judgment. That is superstitious nonsense.

Likewise, if we study success, we can see that it is the result of certain causes. We don't, as rational human beings, blame it on the gods of fortune. That is superstitious nonsense.

What you have as results in your life are effects. What is the cause of these effects? In the ways that count most, you are. It is only when you accept full responsibility for your life that you gain the freedom to be at cause.

People who blame the results in their lives, the effects they experience, on outside events, conditions and circumstances relegate themselves to being mere creatures of circumstance at the mercy of fate.

People who accept responsibility for the effects they get to experience step up to the place of power called being at cause and can therefore assume the godlike ability of being able to determine the flow and shape of their own lives and thereby, create their own destiny.

Once you have accepted the fundamental principle that lies behind all that it means to be human in the universe called Cause and Effect, then you can move on to understanding and applying the other Natural Laws to your life in order to create the success you idealize and desire.

The Eight Major Natural Laws ::

The descriptions that follow will give you some insight into how much potential you have to be consciously creative and how powerful you will become when you learn to "play by the rules" and apply these natural laws to the way you live your life.

Of course there are people who do not consciously know about these Laws and still manage to create success. As I have said before, many times, the secret of power lies not in the knowledge, but in the application. So it is possible for someone to make the direct application without actually having the knowledge. You can light a fire without knowing exactly what processes enable a fire to burn.

But it is better, if you want to be consciously and intentionally creative, to have both the knowledge of how things work and then the will to make the application and put this knowledge to work.

By defining these Natural Laws here and describing how they work, it is my intent to empower you to become capable of creating, for yourself, the life of your dreams. I can only hope that you accept this challenge. It is entirely up to you to apply this information to your own life.

The Law of Comprehensiveness: all is one.

All apparent distinctions, separations, dualities and existent things are united in one grand unifying schema. You may seem to be a distinct thing; but you are inseparable from the whole. That distant star may appear to be completely separate and removed from you; but you are intimately connected to it. Some event that takes place in your world may not immediately be perceived as being directly related to your life; but it is, in fact, a part of who you are.

The uni-verse is one song. Each part of it is a separate note, each adding to the complete harmonic. Even the spaces between the notes are an integral part of the music. It is possible to identify a certain part and call it C-sharp or The Milky Way or Leslie Fieger; but that does not mean that it exists separately from the whole.

You exist within and are an integral part of the universe. All things that exist in our universe are entangled in the same web of energy and consciousness. That includes you. Entanglement is the term used in Quantum Physics to describe the fact that all things, no matter how far apart and separate they may seem to be, are connected at some basic level and thus, when one thing changes, other things also change.

What that means is that when you change your behavior or your way of thinking, the world also changes. Since you are a choice enabled creature, you can make a conscious choice to change yourself and thus have an effect on the universe.

Such is your power.

The Law of Conservation: energy can neither be created nor destroyed.

Everything is energy and cannot be destroyed, only transformed from one state to another as enabled by the Law of Allowingness. Matter is a state of energy. Light is a state of energy. Thought is a state of energy. Motion is a state of energy. Emotion is a state of energy. Since energy cannot be created, almost all your personal acts of creation are simply the conscious and intentional transformation of energy from one state to another.

There is one exception to this law and that is thought energy. Whenever you think a new original thought, you are creating a new wave of energy. This amazing power of the human mind to originate a thought is literally a divine power. Most of the time, most people are not utilizing this power. Their thinking consists of repetitive patterns of old unoriginal thoughts. Nothing new is imagined or conceived of and no new energy is created by this repetitive recycled thinking pattern.

Even focused, intentional thought does not add new energy to the universe. The tremendous power of this type of thought is its power to transform already existing energy from one form to another. (see the Law of Allowingness)

Totally new, original thought, however adds to the totality of the universe. The universe is a sea of energy and any new thought that adds to that sea is new energy.

Your imagination therefore can actually cause the universe to become more. That is how powerful you are. Universal intelligence thought the physical universe into being and you are endowed with the power to create new thoughts and therefore add to the sum total of creation.

Imagine that. Claim your power.

The Law of Harmonics: everything is vibration.

Energy vibrates in certain ways and has certain characteristics, like frequency, periodicity, amplitude, and shape. Frequency and periodicity are the time related aspects of vibration; amplitude and shape are the space related aspects of vibration.

The song of the universe comes together as one grand harmonic. If there was no harmony in the way the various interlocking and interconnecting myriad of vibrations that make up the physical universe interplay with each other, it would not exist. There would be chaos instead of a cosmos.

A wave packet, like a Quark, is a harmonic. Quarks make up protons. Without protons, there would be no atoms, no molecules, no universe. The very existence of the universe depends upon harmonics.

Your body exists because of harmonics. If all the cells of your body did not agree to work together in harmony, conducted by the director whose name is Deoxyribonucleic Acid, you would not be able to have a body.

Your thoughts are vibrations. If they lack harmony, we say they are discordant. When the results that show up in your life are not "in tune with" the ideals you hold for yourself, then it is because your thoughts are discordant, not in harmony with your ideals and not in harmony with Natural Laws.

Since you have the power to choose how and what you think, you are enabled to create a life of harmony and success or… discord and failure. It is up to you.

That is how powerful you are.

The Law of Polarity: everything exists in pairs of opposites.

All energy has polarity. There is negative and positive. We have electricity because we understand the Law of Polarity. Imagine your life without electricity. Try also to imagine life without the polarity of male and female, light and dark, up and down. Impossible.

Nothing would even exist without polarity. Atoms are composed of negative and positive energies, electrons and protons. Protons, themselves are made up of quarks. Quarks come in pairs of polarities, called Up and Down, Strange and Charmed, Top and Bottom.

The Law of Polarity is also evident in magnets. There is a North Pole and a South Pole. Line the magnets up with the north poles all facing one direction and they will be attracted to each other. Place the magnets North Pole to South Pole and they will repel each other. In your life, what you resist will persist because you are not aligning yourself pole to pole, you are attempting to force two opposites together.

In every adversity, there is the polarity of advantage; in every advantage there is the polarity of adversity.

Even though we only exist in this present now moment, we perceive the polarity in time of past and present. That polarity enables us to have memory and to plan for (imagine) the future.

Imagine that, you can create a plan for how the future unfolds for you. What power you have.

The Law of Attraction: like energy is attracted to like energy.

Gravity is a prime example of this Law of Attraction. Stars are born because of this law. Where would you be without a star to hang around? Your world, Planet Earth, is spinning at 1,000 miles per hour. That is a lot of centrifugal force. Why are you not spun off into space? Gravity.

The mass of your body is attracted to the mass of the planet. The basic elements of your body are made of the same elements as the planet. They are alike and are attracted to each other. Matter is energy. Like energy is attracted to like energy.

Everything is composed of energy. Your thoughts are a form of energy. Your thoughts create electrochemical events in your brain. Your neurons spark when you think and this measurable electrical energy is broadcast out from you into your world.

Your emotions are a form of energy. You know that from experience. You can feel a person's anger or fear or love. You are feeling the energy emitted by that other person.

Beliefs are ingrained repetitive thought patterns. They are standing waves of thought energy. Your intentions are purposeful and consistent feelings. They are standing waves of emotional energy.

So, like all forms of energy, your thoughts, beliefs, emotions and intentions attract and are attracted to similar forms of energy.

You attract that which is most like how you are being and behaving.

Since you can choose how and what to think, how and what to believe, how and what to feel and how and what to intend, you can choose to attract into your life any ideal you can create in your imagination.

I stand in awe at your power.

The Law of Allowingness: everything can be transformed from one state to another.

Matter can become energy. Ice can melt to become water; water can boil to become steam. Steam can drive a turbine to produce electrical energy. Energy can become matter. Quantum physics describes how that occurs all the time. Evolution can occur. An example of evolution is that Hydrogen can become Deuterium. So too, can mutation occur. An example of mutation is that Helium can become Carbon. So, too can a unique creation occur. Imagination can become reality. Thoughts can become things.

All things that can be thought of can be made real, be made manifest. If you can think it and believe in it and desire it and intend it, the potential for its manifestation already exists. You do not need to invent the process for it to come into being. It is already there. You may have to discover it, but you do not have to create it.

Whatever exists already in your life can be transformed from what it is to what you idealize.

And, since you can make choices about what ideals to create in your imagination, you have the power to transform your life in each and every present moment.

The Law of Abundance: everything multiplies.

Darn good thing too. Imagine what dire straights we would be in if one kernel of wheat planted yielded only one kernel of wheat as a crop. A single grain of wheat, when planted, will yield about 85 new grains of wheat, 84 of which can be turned into flour with one saved to be re-planted to yield yet another 85 grains.

There would be no need for that campfire to cook your meals without the Law of Abundance.

The universe is expanding. New stars are being created. More people are being born. The original energy released by the Big Bang is still being transformed into more complex forms of matter.

Wealth is the abundance of things valued. Poverty is not a lack of wealth; it is the abundance of the lack of things valued. Problems multiply when you focus your attention on problems. Solutions multiply when you focus your attention on solutions. Obstacles multiply when you focus your attention on obstacles. Opportunities multiply when you focus your attention on opportunities.

Since you have the power to choose where you focus your attention, you have the power to effectuate the Law of Abundance and bring into your life more of the things that you are focusing your attention on.

What exactly are you focusing your attention on these days?

The Law of Compensation: everything is in balance.

There is a cost to everything. Nothing can appear or be made manifest without some transformation taking place that causes the apparent disappearance of some other thing. I say apparent disappearance, because that other state of energy has not actually disappeared; it still exists "in potentia" and the Law of Allowingness will enable it to return if the proper conditions are brought to bear.

Human beings instinctively understand that this Law of Compensation exists and various philosophies attempt to describe it and most societies attempt to impose it in some practical way on its membership. Karma is one way it has been described. Sin and retribution is another way of describing it. Effort and reward is yet another way to describe it. Sowing and reaping is another allegorical way to describe it.

Of course, no god personally punishes you for your sins. That is just the allegorical description of the Law of Compensation. If you jump off the roof of a twenty-three story building, there is nothing personal in gravity pulling you to your death. What is happening in this instance is that your willful ignorance of (or willful compliance with) this variation of the Law of Attraction results in an unpleasant experience.

The Law of Compensation says that there is a price to be paid for every condition. Nothing comes for free. Some price or exchange of energy is required in every case. Every moment of life lived is a moment spent. There is no gain without some loss. There is no loss without some gain. In order to obtain any form of wealth, you must transform some other form of energy into abundance.

Pay with your time or pay with your contribution or pay with your creativity. Masters of the game pay the price of prosperity by thinking new thoughts and creating new ways to express themselves that will add value or benefits for other people, thereby adding to the totality of the universe and the overall wealth of humanity.

Now you have a basic understanding of the rules of the game and how truly powerful you inherently are; and can become when you decide to play by the rules.

Choose now to become empowered and create the success you desire and so richly deserve.

Quick Review:

There are Natural Laws, sometimes called Metaphysical or Spiritual Laws that govern how all things in the universe unfold. All effects have causes. You are a causal being.

Direct Action Steps:

Read the DELFIN Trilogy for a more in depth understanding of Natural Laws and how you cab use this knowledge to become a conscious creator and realize your desired ideals.

"Failing to plan is planning to fail."

~ Benjamin Franklin

"Reduce your plan to writing. The moment you complete this, you will have given definite, concrete form to the intangible desire."

~ Napoleon Hill

"All successful people have a goal. No one can get anywhere unless he knows where he wants to go and what he wants to be or do. "

~ Norman Vincent Peale

Chapter Seven

Charting The Course

Destiny and destination both refer to a place to go or to end up. Neither is attained without first embarking on the journey. Of course, if you just set off on a journey without a destination in mind and without a map to follow or directions on how to get to the destination, you will end up who knows where. This is simple advice, so simple, it should not be even necessary to impart.

Nevertheless, for some reason, that is exactly how most people live their lives... without following a road map or a set of specific directions. Some are offered maps and directions and perversely, refuse or fail to follow the certain path to their stated destination and choose instead to wander around for years, hoping that they will stumble upon their destiny.

That approach may result in some exciting adventures and discoveries of unknown places, but seldom results in arrival at the chosen destination.

In order to successfully arrive at a chosen destination, there are three critical pieces of information you must have:

1. Your point of embarkation. You must know where you are starting from — where you are at. Imagine this scenario... I have made you unconscious and secretly transported you to some unknown place on Earth, in the middle of some jungle. When you wake up, you discover a note and a key. The note explains that the key will open a specific safety deposit box in a certain bank in London. It goes on to explain that there are $100 million in bearer bonds and stock certificates in that safety deposit box that can all be yours. All you have to do is get there within 48 hours. Your fortune awaits you. Your goal is clear... get to London as fast as possible.

What is the very first thing you must figure out?

Yes, you know the answer. You can't get there from here unless you first know where the heck you are. A great many people, who set specific goals about where they want to get to in life, never actually make the effort to figure out where they are starting from.

Without knowing where you are at, it is impossible to chart your journey even with the best of maps.

2. Your destiny. You must also know the location of your destination. If you do not know where London is located, you cannot arrive, except by some very remote chance. But that is just the example. You have not woken up to find that note about the bank in London. You must design your own destiny. You must create your ideals in your own imagination. You must decide where you are going in this journey through life. Unless of course, you are content to wander around aimlessly, hoping to stumble across King Solomon's lost mines.

3. A plotted course or directions. Even if you, in this jungle, were to discover a perfect topological globe of the world with a big read 'X' marking your location, but without roads, towns and airports marked on it and without a compass to guide you, you would likely never escape the jungle. You must have and follow a specific plotted course. You must be able to know what direction you are traveling. OR, you must have a guide who does know the way and you must be willing to follow the guide.

Again, very simple stuff. Strangely, in this journey through life, most people do NOT know where they are at, do NOT have a map to follow (or stubbornly refuse to refer to a map that may have been provided) and do NOT have a clear idea of where they are headed, where their chosen destination is actually located.

Let's see if we can remedy that…

    Embarkation      Destination

I have found that most people are only interested in the map. How do I get there? (You are probably reading this book in the hope that this is the map that will lead you to your success.) People want the arrow, but they don't know where to point it to and they don't know where it is pointing from. They seem to forget, perhaps ignore, that you need to know where *there* is and you also need to know where *here* is.

The first thing you must do after you have defined and envisioneered your success (which is the description of your destination), in order to create your success, is to figure out where you are starting from. Only a fully honest and critical self-evaluation can accomplish that. And that is something that only you can do for yourself.

And then, you must set clear and specific goals. You must know what steps to take as you embark on your journey.

If your ideal is your destination, then the steps along the road to your destination are your specific goals. If your ideal is to travel to Mars, then one of your first goals would be, of necessity to build or procure a spaceship, then another of your goals would be to break free of Earth's gravity well.

Similarly, you cannot just expect to jump straight to the fulfillment of your ideal, you must have specific identifiable intermediate goals. I've heard a lot of talk recently that having specific goals are not necessary; that all you need is the clear powerful intention and the universe will magically supply the means. Nonsense. Drivel. You can't just intend to go to Mars; you need to decide how you are going to get there and then take the necessary steps. These intermediate steps are your specific goals. Without them, you are going nowhere.

Yes, intentions are important. In fact, the intent you bring to everything you do in life is one of critical components of conscious creation. But intentions alone will not produce the specific results you desire. The old proverbial saying that the road to hell is paved with good intentions should serve to remind everyone that you need more than the intention. You need the specific ideal, the profound desire, the intentional thought and action. How do you get intentional actions? By having specific goals… the defined steps on your path.

Millions of words have been written about goal setting. Millions of people set goals. Yet, most goals set by most people remain unfulfilled. I have distilled (from experience and education) the eleven essentials of successful goal setting here for you. Follow these, and you will accomplish your goals. Fail to follow these and you probably will not. No hype. No rah-rah encouragement. No fluff. Just the simple explanation of how and why to set and ACCOMPLISH goals.

1. Your goals must be original

That does not mean that they cannot be the same or similar to the goals that others may have; it means that they must be yours, not second-hand. Many people set goals according to the hopes and expectations that they have been programmed to have by parents, teachers, society and cultural norms.

As a consequence, you do not own these goals. You cannot generally have or hold what is not yours, or, even if you do manage to keep it, it will not have any value or meaning to you. What's the point then of having it? The real reason you set and hope to achieve goals is not just to have the thing idealized, it is to be happy and fulfilled in the accomplishment.

Set goals that are yours; not something inherited or assumed. If they are not your own original goals, even if you do manage to accomplish them, it will mean very little to you. Why waste your life pursuing something that will end up as meaningless?

2. Your goals must be inspirational

They must arouse your passion. This must be a consuming passion, not some whim or "someday I'd like to" feeling. You must desire passionately to achieve what you set as a goal. It must drive you to action and you must feel fulfilled in that action because you know that it is leading to the fulfillment of your goal.

It is passion that drives you to move continuously toward your goal. It is passion that keeps you from getting distracted. It is passion that keeps you from getting discouraged. It is passion that fuels your motivation. It is passion that draws others to you to assist in your goals. It is passion that inspires you and others. It is passion that lights your way through the darkness that you will find along the way.

Get passionate about your goals or get passionate about someone else's. Life without passion is not a life; it is merely an existence.

3. Your goals must be harmonious

Obviously, you cannot have conflicting goals in life or you will be conflicted. That's the easy part. Your goals, however, must also be in harmony with your core beliefs and your self-assigned purpose in life.

It is easy to understand that to have conflicting goals will raise your stress levels and frustrate you. Yet, people do that to themselves all the time.

It is not so easy to understand that you may have some deep-set unconscious game plan for your life (whether from some basic spiritual urge or from some sense of undefined purpose) and the goals you set may actually be in conflict with that real — but hidden — game plan.

First, decide who you are and what you are here to do and then set your goals in alignment with that; or you, yourself, on a subconscious or super conscious level, will continually be sabotaging your goals.

4. Your goals must be realistic

There is not much point in setting a goal to personally live on Mars, if you are today (in 2008 as I write this) over 95. The goals you set for yourself must be achievable within the framework of what is humanly possible.

But (and this is important) realistic does not mean what the majority commonly accepts as realistic. Most people did not think that it was realistic to attempt to fly a bicycle with wings and a motor attached, but two brothers named Wright did. Most people did not think it was realistic to build a personal computer for people to use in their home, but two guys named Steve did.

These 4 guys changed reality for all of us. Their goals were obviously, in retrospect, quite realistic. Don't let your imagination be hemmed in by the crowd.

5. Your goals must be idealistic

They must be idealistic in two ways: they must involve your personal ideals in the five below-mentioned areas of your life and they must be progressively higher or further ahead than you are at now.

Most people are, in some way, in conflict with the different aspects of self:

Material and Financial ($$$ and Things)

Physical and Environmental (Health of Body, Home and World)

Emotional and Relationship (Happiness, Love, Social Contact)

Mental and Educational (Learning, Awareness, Self-Knowledge)

Spiritual and Ethical (Unity, Life Purpose, Values, Sacredness)

If your goals are not in tune with your ideals, you will be conflicted. This is why people without defined personal ideals and specific goals are unhappy and why they do not achieve their highest potential. Set your goals in harmony with your ideals.

If your goals are not idealistic (in the sense that they are progressive), you will get bored and unsatisfied. People (those who don't understand) often wonder why those who are already extremely wealthy continue to pursue more wealth. It is because the ideal is always being extended or raised. Great achievers don't rest on their laurels. Each goal achieved is merely a stepping-stone to more and greater achievement. It is not the end in itself.

6. Your goals must be specific

Goals like, "I want to be rich", are not worth the paper they are printed on. Rich must be defined. One million dollars in the bank might mean rich to most people, but it means poor to many others. It is the same for more ethereal goals. "I want to be happy" means nothing. Happy must be defined just as rich must be defined. "I want to be spiritually fulfilled" is the same; meaningless, unless defined.

What does rich mean to you? Exactly. What does happy mean to you? Don't know? Then how on earth will you ever even know if you get there? I have met a lot of people who say they are on a spiritual path. I like to ask where that path is leading. Most can't say anything specific. It is all very nebulous. If your destination is not defined, how in heaven's name will you know if and when you get there?

7. Your goals must be adaptable

One of my favorite jokes (which would offend some readers so I will not quote it here) involves a guy who had set a specific goal but when a gal came along to offer a much better fulfillment, he asked her to help him to accomplish his original one. Many people miss the better fulfillment of a goal because their focus on the one they had originally visualized is too intense and narrow to recognize the better one when it shows up.

Be sure that you are focused on the best possible fulfillment of your goal, not just on the method that you foresaw that goal fulfillment happening.

8. Your goals must be visualized

If you cannot see it as real and as true and as part of the way you life your life; it will not happen.

Many folks, when confronted with some seemingly outrageous possibility or goal, will comment, "I'll believe it when I see it made real, not just some imaginary ideal". The dreamers, schemers and achievers of history all had a different approach: "I see it. I believe it. It is real if it exists in my imagination."

Tiger Woods 'sees' his shots landing on the green a few feet from the cup before he takes the shot. The average golfer looks up (usually too soon) from his shot to see where it went. Guess whose shots end up where most often. Visualize the reality in your imagination and it will become real in your manifestation.

9. Your goals must be affirmed

You must tell yourself all day, every day, in your constant conscious and subconscious self-talk that your goal is real and achievable. AND, you must tell others what your goal is so that they can 'buy into it' and contribute to it. If you don't believe in it enough to make it a part of your daily conversation and are not passionate enough about it to be compelled to talk about it to yourself and others, it is NOT real for you and it will NOT become real.

You will be surrounded by naysayers. Someone must speak the truth of the reality of your goal. That is YOUR 24/7 job. Constantly affirm where you are headed and why. You'll end up not only convincing yourself but the world as well.

10. Your goals must be time related

Everything exists in space and time. If something is not defined precisely in space and time, it does not exist. A goal of "someday, I'd like to be financially secure", or "someday, I'd like to climb that mountain", does not, and it is highly likely that it WILL NOT, ever, exist as anything other than nebulous, wishful thinking. You must set specific times for your goals to be made manifest OR you will be forever going towards your goals and never quite reaching them.

Almost everyone in developed countries sets the goal of retirement in financial security, but the overwhelming majority do NOT achieve that. Why? One of the reasons is that it is always a 'someday' goal, not a 'by June 21st, 2014' goal. Of course, it is also likely that these people are also not applying the other 10 rules of effective goal setting.

11. Your goals must be written down

If it exists only in your head, it is only wishful thinking. This is the basic, proven by experience, truth of the matter: 95% of people who have specific written goals accomplish them; and 95% of people who have unwritten goals (specific or not) do not.

If you can read that previous sentence and not begin immediately to write down your goals, you might as well resign yourself to the fact that you will not accomplish what you imagine you want to be, do and have in life.

Yes there are those few high achievers who manage to set clear, distinct goals without writing them down and also manage to stay focused on them for their entire lives. Don't kid yourself: you are not one of those people. I'll prove it to you. Tell me (or anyone) right now exactly, specifically, and in full detail what goals you held 1,000 days ago.

Write them down. Period. Now. Chart your course or you will stray off course and not get where you want to be, not get what you want to do and not get what you want to have.

Quick Review:

You can only get where you want to go if you a) know where you are starting from and b) if you have a clearly defined destination and c) have a road map or game plan to get you from a to b.

Direct Action Steps:

Take a cold realistic look at your life. Where are you at materially, physically, emotionally, mentally and spiritually?

	Material & Financial	Physical & Environmental	Emotional & Relationship	Mental & Educational	Spiritual & Ethical
Your current situation					
Your defined ideals					
Your specific goals					
Your Daily To Do List					

Make a detailed and time related list of goals in all five areas of your life: material, physical, emotional, mental and spiritual. Review these every day.

"Your time is limited, so don't waste it living someone else's life. Don't be trapped by dogma - which is living with the results of other people's thinking. Don't let the noise of other's opinions drown out your own inner voice. And most important, have the courage to follow your heart and intuition. They somehow already know what you truly want to become. Everything else is secondary."

~ Steve Jobs

Chapter Eight

Speaking The Truth

All day every day you are talking. Sometimes your mouth is moving when you are speaking, but most of the time it is not.

Huh??? No, it is not because you are a ventriloquist.

All day (and even all night) you are constantly talking to yourself. This self-talk is mostly subconscious background noise that you normally pay no conscious attention to, but that does not diminish its importance in determining your reality.

This self-talk is a constant stream of affirmations about how you perceive the world, what you believe to be true about your world and your place in it, about what is possible for you to be, to do and to have in life.

(You may have discovered by now that there is some repetition in this book. That is intentional. I am helping you to adopt a new prosperity paradigm and your method of self-talk by affirming and re-affirming the essential understandings you must adopt and apply in order to become a consciously creative self-actualized human being.)

When you pay attention to your self-talk and understand that this subconscious programming is determining how you behave and thus what results show up in your life, you will come to see that **when you listen to this subconscious self-talk, you are listening to your future unfold.**

So, in order to change the future that is unfolding for you right now, right here in this present moment, you need to take conscious control of this subconscious self-talk.

Of the approximately 60,000 thoughts that pass through your mind each day, a large percentage is useless trivia like old ad jingles, snippets of old songs and other nonsensical tidbits of information you have been repetitively exposed to in your past. These can be ignored.

What is critical to pay attention to is the recurring self-talk that is about the image you hold of yourself, how you believe that the world works and how you see your place in the world. This is where you must exert your control.

The best method that I know that enables you to effectively do this is a five step process:

      a. Get still for at least twenty minutes.
      b. Pay attention to the stream of thoughts that are passing through your mind. Identify the major repetitive patterns.
      c. Ask yourself the following questions… "Why am I thinking that thought? Where did it come from? Does it serve me in any way to think that way? Can I think differently about that?"
      d. Begin the process of thinking more empowering thoughts by creating specific affirmations about the person you wish to be, the things you aspire to do and the success you envision having.
      e. Have the discipline to repeat these affirmations to yourself throughout the day.

For example, while other people are complaining about standing in line at the bank, I am affirming my ideals repetitively. You'll know when this has begun to work when you find yourself thinking these affirmations without consciously choosing to do so.

The things you habitually talk about to other people are also important. What you talk about defines what you believe in, what you care about, what you are in the process of creating for yourself and how much value you place on your life. Yes, what you talk about demonstrates how much value you place on your life.

If you talk about nothing but inanities, then it is obvious that you place no value on your own time since you are willing to waste it talking about nonsense, and that you place no value on the other person's life since you are willing to waste the precious moments of their life talking about useless stuff and that you place no value on your ability to contribute to the person you are speaking to since all you are willing to talk about are non-contributory things. You have devalued yourself and the other person.

If you listen carefully to what other people speak about, you will soon come to see the truth of that old saying, "Below average people talk about other people; average people talk about things and events; and above average people talk about ideas."

Super successful people spend a lot of time speaking about ideals. What ideals? The ones they create in their own imagination.

To expand upon that simplistic adage so that you can see that how you speak and what you say demonstrate what your thought processes are mostly about and how you are constantly defining your potential and constructing your reality, think about the following ideas.

You can tell a lot about people by what they read. What people read is one of the ways they talk to themselves and reinforce (affirm) how their reality picture is constructed. One of the first things I do, and have done for years, when invited to someone's home or office is to look at their bookshelves (if they have any) and at any magazines they have lying around.

What I have learned from this observation is that interesting people have interests that empower them and uninteresting people have interests that disempower them.

If a person's reading material consists of National Inquirer, People Magazine or any of their equivalents, you know that they have low self-esteem and any conversation you will have with them will be more gossip than anything else and they will be disempowering to themselves and you.

If a person's reading material consists mainly of daily newspapers and magazines like Time, Newsweek, The Economist, et cetera, you know that any conversation with them will consist of world events and prevailing conditions in the world because they believe that they are creatures of event and circumstance and they will be disempowering to themselves and you.

If a person's reading material consists of magazines like The Atlantic and New Scientist, or websites like closertotruth.com or TED.com, you know that any conversation with them will be interesting and intelligent and they will be empowering to themselves and you.

If a person's bookshelf has books like this one or books by Wayne Dyer, Deepak Chopra, Amit Goswami, et cetera, you know that they are interested in personal growth and empowerment and, as a consequence, will have something valuable to say and they will be empowering to themselves and you.

A person who does not read good books is no better off than a person who cannot read. A person who is not continually learning is no better off than the child in some impoverished country who has no access to education.

A person who fills their mind with trash cannot realistically expect to have a happy, successful and fulfilling life. Yet, many people are constantly filling their minds with trash. How? By having conversations with themselves that reinforce a worldview that does not empower, by having conversations with others about banalities, trivialities and inanities, by reading trash or by not reading at all and by watching junk on television.

I do not even own a television. It is not just because there is nothing worth watching most of the time; but the fact that the majority of the stuff that is broadcast is actually designed to disempower the audience. It makes you stupid.

If you think you are immune, you are deluding yourself. Television is a combination of narcotic and mind viruses. It puts you into an alpha brainwave state and then dumps garbage into your subconscious mind. It is not entertainment; it is entrainment.

Turn off your television and turn on your inner vision and you will become empowered to take control of your own life, your own success and your own freedom.

Start having conversations with people that are empowering. Instead of asking them about who won the ball game, ask them how they plan on winning the game of life. Instead of telling them the latest gossip, tell them what you are creating.

Don't spend too much time talking about what is already manifest, what already exists. That just makes you average. Allow other people to live their lives. Don't waste your time talking about them unless you want to be below average.

Talk about your truth, your ideals, what you desire to see manifest. Talk about these things to yourself and to others. When you speak about your ideals (your truth) with passion to other people, they will get enthused about helping you achieve your ideal. You will also inspire them to live larger lives.

You only have two really valuable assets: the time you were given (& use wisely); the ideals you create (& strive to enact). All else is of lesser import. So why spend your mental energy, your time and your attention on things that are not relevant to the person you desire to become, the ideals you desire to enact and the success you desire to attain.

Learn to replace that constant mental chatter, those endless tape loops of old ad jingles, self-defeating self-talk and subconscious non-productive mental patterns with new, bold, empowering affirmations about who you are becoming, what you are in the process of creating and the gratitude you have for having these ideals be a part of your reality.

Speak always, first and foremost, your own truth.

Otherwise, you'll end up living somebody else's.

Quick Review:

You can take conscious control of the subconscious thought patterns that control how you behave and what you expect life to be like.

Everything you talk about, to yourself and others, is an affirmation of the person you are in the process of becoming.

Direct Action Steps:

Turn off your television.

Start paying attention to your thought processes.

Make a list of specific affirmations that support the new you and your ideals.

Train yourself to think intentionally and creatively.

Learn something new everyday.

"A little knowledge that acts is worth infinitely more
than much knowledge that is idle."
~ Kahlil Gibran

"I have always thought the actions of men the best
interpreters of their thoughts."
~ John Locke

"Good thoughts are no better than good dreams,
unless they be executed!"
~ Ralph Waldo Emerson

"In any moment of decision the best thing you can do
is the right thing,
the next best thing is the wrong thing,
and the worst thing you can do is nothing."
~ Teddy Roosevelt

Chapter Nine

Acting The Part

There are those who preach that writing positive affirmations and sticking them on the fridge door will, by itself, magically produce health, wealth and happiness.

Although this is a very good and effective way to change the way you think and take on more empowering beliefs, it is not a magic pill that will, by itself produce results.

Let me be very plain. Actions alone produce results.

Knowledge, understanding and wisdom can teach you the best way to act and thus produce better results; but knowledge alone, understanding alone and wisdom alone do not produce tangible material results. It requires action to produce results.

It is necessary to do before you can have. Of course, you are empowered to do more or behave in a better, a more effective way, when you have more knowledge and understanding, but you still must take action before anything actually happens. You can have the most glorious vision of a mansion in your mind, but unless you actually build a roof, the rain will still fall on your head.

Maybe, if you are some super enlightened soul, like the almost mythical Babiji, you can sit in some cave in the Himalayas and manifest all kinds of things without doing the doing that the real world expects; but I am not capable of that magic and I suspect that you are not either, so do not pretend otherwise. It is fantasy to expect that you can be still and not do anything and somehow, produce an ideal life. You must take action.

I have written much about how, in order to have more of what we desire in life, we must first do more and, that, in order to do more, we must first become more. In fact, the focus of the majority of my articles and books is about how to become more. I reiterate, time and time again, how important it is to acquire the specific knowledge of success if you want to have the success you desire.

I also make it a point to emphasize that knowledge alone is not power; that it is applied knowledge (or action) that provides the personal power to create. Nevertheless, I get many emails from people telling me that they have spent years studying and learning the metaphysical principles of success, without having any demonstrable increase in abundance, prosperity or material success. "Why?" they ask does this stuff not work for me.

In most cases, after some direct discussion, I find it is because these people are not actually doing the necessary things to make a practical application of their education.

Just as you can obtain a degree in medicine, but cure no illness or save no lives if you do not actually work at being a doctor; you can know all the principles of success, but if you do not actually put them into practice, they will not work to produce results for you. You must act.

You can, for example, fully understand how the Law of Attraction works and you can have a harmonious mental attitude; but, if you want to create material abundance or financial success and you do not enact what you know by applying it *within the available and proven ways* to produce success, then your knowledge and education is wasted.

Mark Twain once commented that people who do not read good books are no better off than people who cannot read. I will elaborate on that to say that people who know, **but do not apply**, the knowledge of the conscious and intentional creation of success are no better off than those who are ignorant of the possibilities open to them.

Many people mistake the self-satisfaction they get from acquiring knowledge as being sufficient unto itself. It is, perhaps, enough, if your only goal is to become more educated. It is not enough, however, if your goal is to use that education to produce measurable effects in your personal world.

Financial abundance, or success, is attained, not just because you know certain things, but when you also DO certain things. Things like applying money management techniques. Things like creating or providing valuable goods or services that people will pay you to obtain. Things like marketing your goods and services so that people will know what value you have to offer.

Prove your understanding of the metaphysical principles of success and creation by taking action.

If you have, or represent, a product or service that would appeal to a certain segment of society, then use your understanding of the Law of Attraction in your marketing activities. Don't expect those people who want and need what you have to offer to just somehow find you. Your harmonious vibrations won't stand out that much amongst all the noise and commotion of the world unless you do the necessary marketing.

Enhanced or advanced knowledge and education produces an enhanced ability to perform; but it is the performance, your actions, that produce the results (or circumstances or effects) in your life. Your actions do speak louder than your words. Don't just tell me, or the world, what you know and understand; SHOW me and the world by enacting that knowledge in practical, result-producing, ways.

The ultimate value (and proof) of what you know is in the application or use of that knowledge. Do the doing and you will produce results. Face up to the fact that if the results you have in life are not to your liking, then it is likely that your doing is incorrect. If you don't know what to do to create success, then get the knowledge of success; but don't stop there, do something about it. Make the application.

Of course, indiscriminate action is not an effective way to produce your desired results. You can run around like crazy, climb 100 mountains, cut down forests full of trees and be generally frenetic enough to power up a small city without producing the exact results you wish to have.

You must do the correct things in the correct way. That is why you must get the knowledge... so that you will know what to do. Become more, so that you are capable of more. Then, do more of what needs doing. Then, and only then, will you get to have more of what you want.

I'll say it another way... enlightened actions produce desired results. Understanding how things work is not enough. You must also do the things that work.

You can sit and stare at your navel all you want, but if you don't actually pull the lint out, it will still be there tomorrow.

Yes, you absolutely must take the time and have the discipline to do the inner work first; but in the end, you must take deliberate, consistent and intentional action if you want to produce the results.

The formula is: Become > Enact > Attain.

>**Become what you need to be
>in order to
>Enact what needs to be done
>in order to
>Attain what you desire to have.**

Quick Review:

Knowledge alone is not power. It is the direct and specific application of knowledge that empowers.

Direct Action Steps:

Create a daily to do list each night before going to bed. Review it throughout the day.

"When you follow your bliss... doors will open where you would not have thought there would be doors, and where there wouldn't be a door for anyone else."

~ Joseph Campbell

Chapter Ten

Following Your Bliss

Everyone likes to feel good. You don't eat that piece of chocolate cheese cake because it is good for you. You eat it because for a few moments, you get to feel good.

That beer buzz while watching the ball game on the boob tube does not add any value to your life, but it gives you a feel good fix.

If you are honest with yourself about what motivates you to do almost everything you do in life, you will discover that you are looking for ways to feel good or to cover up some basic sense of unease in your life.

Unfortunately, almost everything that most people do in order to feel good is only a temporary fix. Whether you are shooting a needle full of heroin up your arm or shopping for that new pair of shoes or listening to some motivational talk, or even reading this book, the feel good feeling will soon pass and you will be left needing that next hit. Sound familiar?

There is, however, a way to feel good more often and more consistently without having to resort to these false and, at times, even destructive ways of seeking pleasure.

In Chapter Two, I mentioned that your feelings can be used as a kind of guidance system. When you are not feeling good, you can use that as an indication that you are not living your purpose and your passion; and, instead of looking for some temporary fix that is really only a distraction from your malaise, you can instead look for the real solution, which is to become ever more self-actualized and on purpose with how you live your life.

The ability to be happy is, to a large degree, dependent upon the level of personal fulfillment you can achieve from self-actualization.

A self-actualized person does not need to go looking for things outside of themselves in order to feel good. They know that happiness is available at any time, no matter what external events and circumstances are occurring.

Self-actualization is not a destination; it is a continuous process. Humans are ever more capable of learning, of becoming more, of using more of their talents and skills, of discovering new ways to express themselves.

Self-actualizing people have certain attributes that enable them to experience greater levels of happiness. And, of course, these are attributes that you can choose to take on yourself.

I have listed here the top ten attributes of self-actualized people for you to consider owning and practicing. If you will work each day at taking these on in ever greater implements, you will soon find yourself feeling good about yourself, feeling good about how life is unfolding for you and feeling good about what you are in the process of becoming and creating.

1. Acceptance. Self-actualizing people have greater levels of self-acceptance. They are not in denial about their flaws and weaknesses and do not feel guilty about their errors and omissions. Instead, they work at improving their way of being.

Self-actualizing people also are more accepting of others and tend to recognize that the shortcomings they see in other people are also, to some degree, present in themselves.

2. Reverence. They have greater levels of self-esteem. Even though they recognize and accept their own imperfections, they honor themselves as being sacred creatures and have an innate sense of respect for themselves and their ideals.

Self-actualizing people also honor the sacredness of all other people and of all creation. They recognize that, at some essential level, they are connected to all things.

3. Perception. They have a clearer sense of what is important and what is trivial. They are able to stand back and look at themselves, their thoughts, beliefs, feelings and their actions. They can be the observer as well as the enactor.

Self-actualizing people are able to stand back from the events and circumstances of life and see them for what they are... transitory happenings that do not change the greater reality which is the destiny they have set for themselves.

4. Honesty. They don't tend to hide behind some mask or false identity. They are willing to be themselves in front of other people and do not attempt to live up to the expectations of other people.

Self-actualizing people also do not deceive themselves about themselves or about the reasons for their actions.

5. Individuality. They are not conformists. Although, they may not appear to be non-conformists, they have

learned to think for themselves and have opted out of the crowd mentality.

Self-actualizing people don't accept other people's opinions or the news at face value. They recognize propaganda when they see it and understand that they must be vigilant in maintaining freedom of thought and belief.

6. Commitment. They are committed to living a full and meaningful life and know that by creating ideals and setting specific goals, they are taking charge of and honoring their own life.

Self-actualizing people are also committed to making a difference in the lives of others through the contributions that they make by their creativity and commitment.

7. Motivation. They are self-motivated and do not need to have constant outside stimuli in order to feel inspired to take action. They use what they are passionate about to motivate themselves.

Self-actualizing people are also motivating forces in other people's lives, often inspiring others to perform at higher levels than they would normally. Their own passion ignites a fire in other people.

8. Appreciation. They are grateful for all that life has to offer. Problems become opportunities to grow. Opportunities therefore abound. Obstacles become challenges to gain power. Challenges produce rewards. Rewards become blessings to celebrate. Blessings multiply. Achievements become milestones on the continuous road to success. Milestones become the legacy, the gift they leave behind for others to emulate or to take inspiration from.

Self-actualizing people are also appreciative of the contributions of others and express their gratitude, not just verbally but by demonstrating their appreciation through direct contribution to the other person's life.

9. Mystical. They not only have a sense of the sacredness of all things, including their own dreams and ambitions, they have at times a mystical sense of unity with all other people, with all things, with all of creation. This sense of unity or peak mystical experience induces a sense of wonder and a sense of personal power to be at cause.

Self-actualized people are often inspired to share those mystical experiences with others because they have come to know that this sense of unity with all things is the greater reality than the day-to-day events and circumstances of life.

10. Imagination. They are envisioneers. They practice creative envisioneering because they know that the creative power of the human mind is the source of all wealth, happiness and personal power and fulfillment. They are therefore very creative people.

Self-actualized people share their vision with other people, not just to get them to assist in the actualization of that vision; but also to teach through action that everyone can be creative and can design a life of success, constant growth and attainment.

So, if you want to feel good now and feel even better tomorrow, instead of running off to the ice cream store for some extra chocolate or instead of turning on that idiot box to watch some stupid comedy show or instead of running off to some motivational seminar to hear some hyperactive speaker yelling "You can do it!" or

"Halleluiah!"; simply, but progressively, begin the process of becoming a self-actualized human being.

You'll feel a lot better just making the decision to do that. And each day that you work at it, you will feel better and better.

If you really truly want to be happy, then you need to know that true happiness is not to be found in having more. There is no great happiness to be found in owning more stuff, in having more money, in working your way up the corporate ladder, even in accomplishing more.

The secret to true happiness is to be found in the process of ever becoming more self-actualized and in the process of discovering new and better ways to be a contribution.

The late, great Dr. Albert Schweitzer once said, **"Success is not the key to happiness. Happiness is the key to success. If you love what you are doing, you will be successful. I don't know what your destiny will be, but one thing I do know: the only ones among you who will be really happy are those who have sought and found how to serve."**

So, now that you know the secret to feeling good and the secret to being happy, let's go beyond that and talk about how to experience joy and bliss. Wouldn't you love to have a life filled with joy and bliss instead of unease and dissatisfaction? Of course you would.

The title of this chapter is called Follow Your Bliss. I almost did not call it that. I thought about calling it something else, like "Becoming Joyful".

So many authors, coaches and speakers proffer the advice first offered by Joseph Campbell to "follow your bliss"; and so many people take that advice to heart, but are unable to discover what their bliss actually is and, consequently, in the end, just end up being more frustrated with themselves. I therefore seriously hesitated to use this cliché. In the end, I decided to use the title and provide you with some real ways to discover your bliss and to feel joyful.

I cannot tell you what your bliss is; neither can anyone else. That is your job. Only you know that secret passion that your soul holds. Only you can know what gives you joy. Only you know what will light up your life and inspire you to greet each day with a joyous expression of gratitude for the opportunity to play yet another day in this wondrous game called "life on planet earth"; the place in space and time where you get to create, to experience and to share the awesome uniqueness that is you.

While I cannot tell you what your bliss is, perhaps I can help you discover it.

Before we look at how you can discover your bliss, let's take a look at what will happen to you when you begin to follow your bliss.

You will experience a clarity of vision like never before. It will seem as if you had just come out of a cloud bank and into a bright sunny day. The path before you shines clearly and any doubt about what direction you are heading fades away like the fog.

You will experience a sense of timelessness. You will feel totally present in each moment and each moment will be the perfect moment. You will be in the flow like an athlete who is experiencing a peak performance moment.

You will experience being in the right place at the right time and synchronicities will happen like never before. The resources, the ideas, the people you need will just show up as if by magic.

You will experience an expression of your talents like never before. People will be amazed at the wonderful things you are able to express and are able to accomplish.

You will become charismatic and you will take on an aura of purpose and success. Other people will know that you know what you are about.

You will become more insightful, more intuitive and ideas will come to you as if your mind is on fire. Inspiration will bloom in your mind and your heart will overflow with a feeling of joy.

You will be in love.

That is the place you want to be. You can sense that it is available to you. You've been there before. Perhaps not since you were a child, but the residual, cellular memory is still there and it resonates with you. That feeling of bliss is still there for you to rediscover and to follow.

Take a good, long and honest look into your heart and discover what inspires you and what cranks up your passion level. Once you have found that essential truth about yourself, you can go about living a life of purpose and meaning and you will feel good, perhaps even be joyful, most moments of most days.

You may have to go back to your childhood to find that inner place where your secret passion resides. Most adults have suppressed their deep inner desires and passions in order to do what they have thought as necessary in order to survive and prosper in life.

Perhaps, as an adult, you did find something or way of being that gave you that greater sense of meaning and passion, but you did not allow yourself to pursue it because logic or conditioning told you that it was not practical. Go back and find it. Follow the thread of your innermost feelings.

You have unique talents and skills, a unique perspective, unique contributions to make and a unique way of being in the world. Why then, would you allow yourself to be just another cog in the machine? Be you!

Being the real you will produce the bliss. What is the real you? Only your own heart can answer that. Look deep into your heart and find your soul's longing. Then follow that.

And, living in a state of profound gratitude and appreciation will produce joy. Learn to see all things as being sacred. All things include you and your ideals, hopes, dreams and ambitions. They are a measure of your own sacredness and your own divinity. Claim them.

Quick Review:

You will feel good when you are following your bliss, living your passion and being on purpose.

Don't look for that feel good feeling in useless distractions. Look instead to become an intentional person who is on the path to becoming more, enacting more and achieving more. Settle for more.

Direct Action Steps:

Begin today to start taking on the attributes of self-actualizing people. Make it your daily task to consciously and intentionally work towards becoming ever more self-actualized.

"Self-actualizing people, those who have come to a high level of maturation, health and self-fulfillment, have so much to teach us that sometimes they seem almost like a different breed of human beings."

~ Abraham Maslow

"What good is a road map with a destination clearly marked if you do not know where you are starting from? And, of what purpose is the desire to become more if you do not understand who you are already?"

~ Leslie Fieger

Chapter Eleven

Mirror, Mirror

For over a thousand years, people went to the Oracle at Delphi for insight, wisdom and even prophecy.

Socrates, Plato, Pythagoras, Archimedes and Alexander the Great all visited Delphi.

Today, the Oracle is relegated to a footnote in history, classified as Greek Mythology; but to the people of that time, it was as important as the Google search engine combined with the Philosophy Department at the University of Berkeley. If you wanted to know something important or to access the wisdom of the ages, you needed to go to Delphi.

Inscribed over the entrance to Delphi were these words, *"Know Thyself"*.

The great Socrates, to whom, together with his student Plato, we owe much of our western philosophical foundations, took these two words, *"Know Thyself"* as his primary maxim and it was the cornerstone of all his works. His famous saying, "an unexamined life is not worth living," is demonstrative of his belief in the importance of self-knowledge.

Pythagoras, the great mathematician, father of modern geometry and metaphysician said, *"Know thyself - and thou shall know all the mysteries of the gods and of the universe."*

Lao Tzu, the great Chinese sage and author of the Tao Te Ching, wrote, *"Knowing others is intelligence; knowing yourself is true wisdom. Mastering others is strength; mastering yourself is true power."*

According to the Buddha, self-reflection (self-knowledge) was the only dependable way to wisdom and enlightenment.

The Catholic theologian, St. Augustine, said that the only way to transcend the limitations brought on by sensory perceptions of the material, transient world and to comprehend the unity and beauty of all creation was through **self-reflection**.

The great American philosopher, Ralph Waldo Emerson, wrote that, "What lies behind us and what lies before us are tiny matters compared to what lies within us."

And, the Victorian poet, Alfred Lord Tennyson, wrote, "Self-reverence, self-knowledge, self-control; these three alone lead one to sovereign power."

Ayn Rand wrote that a person needs to acquire knowledge of external reality and **self-knowledge** in order to discover and choose his values, goals, and actions.

Millions of books about success are sold each year.

Most people, perhaps including you, who buy these books are looking for the road map that leads to success, are searching for that best, proven method to become more in order to fulfill their desire to have more of all that life has to offer.

I have written this book to provide you with both the map and the method; but the first and most important step of your journey is to Know Yourself as you are; and, to know where you are at right now, where you are starting from and why you are embarking on this journey to a chosen destination called success.

So how do you come to know yourself? First, you simply redirect your attention from the external world of event and circumstance to the internal world of thought, feeling and belief.

You must learn the discipline to spend time with yourself, by yourself, every day in order to stay in touch with the evolving you. Meditation is your best method to do that.

What good is a road map with a destination clearly marked if you do not know where you are starting from? And, of what purpose is the desire to become more if you do not understand who you are already?

If you desire to have success, to be happy and fulfilled, to find meaning and purpose in life, then you must get to know the real you and where you are at currently.

So, let me ask you a question… who are you?

I love to ask people that question. The most common answer I get is, I am John Smith or whatever name they call themselves. My answer is, well, that is your name, but who exactly are you?

Sadly, most people cannot answer that question. Can you?

So, who exactly are you? When you look in the mirror, are you that physical body?

No!

You have a body. It is not you; it is something you have. You already know this. So does almost every thinking person. You body is like your name. It is not you. It is just something you have.

Yet, most people will still say things like "I am sick," when their body is undergoing some process. Your body is the vehicle that enables you to get around on Planet Earth and participate in the many physical experiences available here. Imagining that you are the vehicle is as silly as thinking that your identity is tied to your car. (A common foolishness indulged in by many young men who imagine their own value is enhanced by the sexiness of their vehicle.)

You are not the home you live in, not the clothes you wear, not the car you drive, nor the body you have. You are not your job, not your role in society and not what other people expect you or perceive you to be.

These are just things you do or have. If you do less and have less than me, does that mean that you are less than me? No, you are the same basic essence that I am.

So, if you are not these things that you do or that you have, who exactly are you? When you look in the mirror, are you the mind that observes the body you see?

No!

You have a mind. It is not you; it is something you have. If you stop and ask yourself, "Who am I?", the question is formed in your mind (perhaps even answered); but who is it that is asking the question? The mind is simply the tool you use to ask the question. It is not you. It is not your essence.

So, what is the essence of you? Is it simply your awareness of self? If so, what are you aware of being? If your awareness increases, does that mean that you become more?

If that is so, then perhaps I can enhance your awareness. Let's first take a look at your physical beingness.

Your body is a miracle. It is made up of 75 trillion individual cells (maybe you have an extra billion or so in that spare tire you carry around), each with a defined job function, and all working together harmoniously to provide you a great place to hang out and enjoy the multiple trips around the sun that you get to take whilst working a job, getting married and having offspring.

These cells, in turn, are made up of recycled multi-billion year old stardust. We are carbon-based creatures. Carbon molecules are created in the nuclear furnaces we call stars when 3 helium molecules are fused. When these stars exploded or went super nova, these carbon molecules were distributed in space and then came back together in our planet and ultimately in the life forms that came to inhabit this planet, which, of course, includes you.

According to our latest and greatest understandings of physics and cosmology, all the sub-atomic particles, atoms and molecules that exist in the entire universe were created in the big bang event. So, therefore, every element that exists in your body existed at the genesis of the universe; which means that **the molecular memory of your body extends back in time to the very beginnings of the universe.** Additionally, all the elements that make up your body will survive the demise of your body and will be recycled into another use in the ongoing evolution of the universe.

So, while your personal physical beingness may be a transitory event, the elements that comprise your body are as old and ageless as the universe. You just may not have been aware of that fact before I brought it to your attention. So, now that your awareness is enhanced, is your conception of who you really are enhanced as well?

But, as I said earlier, despite how miraculous it may be, you are not your physicality. It is only an aspect of your total beingness.

Let's take a look a look at that other wondrous aspect of the miracle of you: your mind.

Your mind can envision and contain the entire universe. Maybe you don't spend a lot of time conceptualizing the universe, but Stephen Hawking does. His mind is a human mind, just as is yours; and the human mind is complex enough to do just that. If your mind can potentially envision the entire universe, then it can certainly envision all the success you desire.

It is the human mind that has first conceived of and then created the computer I am using to write this book, conceived and created the International Space Station that floats in space some 200 plus miles above my head as I sit here writing, conceived and created the Internet (that is accessed by and connects one billion people) where I found out the altitude of the space station and where you can find just about all of the accumulated knowledge of humankind. Imagine that.

If, as is said, knowledge is power (at least potential power), then you are more powerful than every single human being from previous generations who has ever lived on this planet. Why? Simply because you have access to more knowledge than the kings, moguls and philosophers of previous ages. You also live in a time when the average person in developed countries enjoys more wealth and comfort than the kings of old.

It is the human mind that also creates all the wealth we enjoy as a species or as individuals. It is your mind that will create the success, wealth and personal fulfillment you will get to experience and enjoy as you travel through life and around the sun as it, in turn, travels through space and time.

Just imagine how fortunate you are: you have access to more knowledge, greater technology, more understanding about how the human mind works than the billions of people who lived before AND more than the majority of people who are alive now. Your potential is limited only by your imagination and those nasty limiting paradigms I wrote about in the Preface.

So, here you are, alive in the best time ever to create wealth and success for yourself, knowing full well that your mind is capable of creating almost anything you can imagine. (The famous quote by Napoleon Hill is truer today than it was when he first wrote it. "Whatever the mind of man can conceive and believe, it can achieve.") Yet, you have not achieved all you desire. Why?

Perhaps, it is because you are not making proper use of your mind. If, you can achieve whatever you can conceive and believe, then it may be possible that the vagueness of the ideals you hold and the limiting beliefs you have are defining (limiting) your ability to create that success.

What are your predominant thought patterns? Why are you thinking what you think? To what end or purpose do you think the way you think? What are your beliefs about your ability to create success and your deservedness to have great wealth? Maybe it is time to think different thoughts and to choose to adopt bigger, better beliefs. Your immediate response to these questions might tell you that you are limiting your own success.

Please answer the following questions honestly. Nobody is listening except you.

Do you believe that you deserve to have all the success and wealth you desire? Or do you believe that you are not good enough, smart enough or educated enough to have a truly abundant and luxurious life?

Do you believe that the potential to create wealth is unlimited? Or limited only by your imagination? Or, like most people, do you believe that there is a limited supply and that when one person has more, it means others must have less?

Allow me to tell you a story about how a belief can limit your success. This past Saturday, I went down to a favorite beach bar to socialize with friends. I ran into a lady who I have known for the past two years. She is a bright, creative, caring and pleasant person, who, like most people, gets by with a comfortable life, but does not have any great level of success in her business or personal life.

She asked me what new projects I was working on (after I had asked her the same question) and when I replied that I was working with a group of people to help them become millionaires within one year, she said, "Wouldn't it be nice to live in a world where no one wanted to become a millionaire?"

I replied, "Wouldn't it be better to live in a world where everyone was a millionaire?" She then explained to me that it was people's drive to have more that was destroying our environment and causing poverty amongst the world's poor. Whoa. Big limiting belief.

Let's take a closer look at what she said…

- The pie is limited. If you have more, I have less.
- The more you have, the more damage you cause.
- Rich people are morally inferior. It would be a sin for her to want more.

It is easy to see that she will never achieve any great levels of success because she believes that it is morally wrong to want more. She definitely does not have a prosperity paradigm.

Most people are not aware that these same subconscious control mechanisms are limiting their own ability to enjoy a prosperous and fulfilling life. Until and unless you examine your own assumed beliefs about wealth and your deservedness, you will not be free to discard these limiting beliefs.

Now, let's take a close look at the reality, not the prejudice.

Wealth is created when someone creates value for others. This value can be either real or perceived; but it is, nevertheless, value that someone (or many people) appreciates and is prepared to pay for.

Wealthy people create more value for more people than poor people. That is how simple it is. Rich people don't take anything away from other people. They contribute in some way to the quality of the lives of others.

The pie is not limited by anything except human imagination. There is more wealth in the world today than ever before, despite the fact that there are more humans alive today than ever before to share in that pie. The pie is actually constantly expanding because wealth is created by the adding of value.

Wealth brings power to effectuate change. Wealthy people contribute more to the betterment of their fellow humans than the poor or middle class. Was that university section or hospital wing built by the underprivileged? Do the middle class attend those thousand dollar charity fundraising dinners?

It is no surprise to learn that rich people individually give more money to charity than average. They can afford to. What is interesting is that the percentage of people donating to charity rises steadily as income brackets increase.

The following figures are extracted from a very detailed and complex study done by James Andreoni and John Sholz of the University of Wisconsin and William Gale of The Brookings Institute.

92% of people earning more than $75,000 per year contribute money to charity, compared to an average of 68% of people who earn less than $75,000 per year. That's money. What about time? 48% of people who earn more than $75,000 per year volunteer their time to charitable organizations. 33% of people who earn less than $75,000 per year volunteer their time.

Merrill Lynch reports that individuals who had a net worth of $1 million or more donated an estimated total of $285 billion to charity in 2006. Millionaire entrepreneurs donated an average of $232,206.00, more than double the amount dedicated to philanthropy by those who inherited their riches.

So, it is easy to see the truth... people who create wealth for themselves contribute to the overall wealth of humanity by the very act of becoming wealthy, creating value and expanding possibilities for others; but they also contribute more of their own money and time to bettering the lives of the less fortunate.

So my lady friend's belief that rich people are taking away from other people is exactly the opposite of the truth. They are, in fact, giving more to other people, in many ways, than the average person. Her belief does not change the facts. Her belief only limits her own ability to be a bigger contribution.

She would be (and so will you be) much better able to improve the situation on this planet by creating success instead of thinking about how much inequity there exists in the world. The best way to improve the world is to improve yourself. Become more. Adopt the Prosperity Paradigm.

An important part of getting to know yourself and then to become more is to take a good close look at what beliefs you might be holding that are limiting your ability to create more success for yourself and thus be able to make a greater contribution to others.

If you want to know the real you and desire to become all you are capable of becoming, start by asking yourself the following questions...

1. Who am I really?
2. Am I living up to my potential?
3. Why not?

4. What beliefs do I have that limit my ability to create massive success?
5. What predominant thought patterns do I have that limit my ability to create more?
6. What feelings do I have about myself that limit my ability to shine my light brighter?
7. Do I have the will to make the personal changes I need to make in order to become more?
8. Why have I not implemented the specific action steps that will lead to success?

Tough questions to be sure; but once you have the personal integrity to answer these questions in complete honesty, you will know where you are at, the point of your embarkation on your journey to the greater you that you deserve to be.

This book can then serve as your roadmap, your guidebook, your map and your compass that will lead you inexorably to your destination... that definition of success that you have created for yourself.

Always remember that you are who you imagine yourself to be. How grand a being can you imagine yourself to be?

What image of yourself do you hold in your imagination? Look in the mirror of self-reflection. What do you see? Who is looking?

Once you decide who you are, then you can decide who you wish to become.

If you are not constantly becoming more, then you are, in fact unbecoming.

You are the grand creator of your own life. Make it your masterpiece.

You will find that life offers you prosperity as soon as the true, inner, powerful, real you uses your will to create a congruency of ideal (vision), word (thought), passion (belief) and deed (action). It really is up to you. Take responsibility now for your life.

Quick Review:

Step one on the path to self-mastery is self-knowledge. Step one on the journey to success is to know and accept where you are currently at. Once you have done that, you can design the plan that will take you to creating and living a super successful life. Commit to becoming more.

Direct Action Steps:

Here is a list of simple, effective things that you can do starting immediately to get control of your life and start consciously and intentionally creating the kind of life you both desire and so richly deserve to have.

1. Spend daily time in reflection, contemplation, meditation, stillness and silence. Ground yourself in self-awareness.
2. Work at gaining control of the physical, emotional, mental and spiritual aspects of self.
3. Develop a strong self-image. Get to know yourself. You are an exceptional individual. You are unique in the whole universe. You are special. You are sacred. Learn to love yourself.
4. Think for yourself. Opt out of mass consciousness. Utilize your creative imagination.
5. Live fully in this present moment. Imagine your ideal future. Make it real.
6. Develop that attitude of gratitude. Be appreciative.
7. Focus your attention on the ideals you have created for yourself.

Epilogue

The Formula

Most people have it all backwards.

They think that if they have certain things (education, opportunities, money, connections, tools, experience); then they can take the right steps (utilize their education, take advantage of the opportunities, invest the money, leverage their connections, make use of the tools, use their experience) and, as a result be successful.

Even many of the so-called personal development gurus and success coaches get it wrong.

They will tell you that the success formula is: 1) get the right information, 2) put it to work in your life and 3) you will be successful. It almost makes sense, doesn't it? But it is not. This is backwards. The formula is not have, then do in order to be. This is like swimming upstream. Wouldn't you rather go with the natural flow of things?

The formula is, and always has been… Be > Do > Have.

I prefer to say it this way because it is a continuous progression: Become > Enact > Attain.

> **Become what you need to be**
> **in order to**
> **Enact what needs to be done**
> **in order to**
> **Attain what you desire to have.**

Everyone clamors for more; more stuff, more money, more success, more satisfaction, more acclaim, more fulfillment, more happiness, more love. Now you know that the secret is that **in order to have more, you must first become more.**

How do you become more?

Who you are depends upon what you think about all day long, what you believe to be true about yourself and your world, how you feel about yourself and your place in the world and what level of intentionality you bring to bear on everything that you do.

So, in order to become more, learn to think bigger and better thoughts, learn to place your attention on the ideals you create, rather than on the passing events and circumstances of everyday life; learn to adopt empowering beliefs about your potentiality and about the possibilities that are available to you; learn to respect and honor yourself and learn to be passionate about your ideals; and learn to always be on purpose instead of allowing yourself to get distracted from becoming, enacting and attaining ever more.

Create a grand new Prosperity Paradigm for yourself and for your world. The world needs you to be successful. When you adopt the Prosperity Paradigm for yourself, you also create a new vibrational pattern in the collective unconscious of all humanity and thereby, you make it possible for more people to become capable of achieving their own success and abundance.

So, go ahead and create that massive success you have always dreamt about. You deserve it.

Leslie Fieger
June 21, 2008

Appendix One

Maslow's Hierarchy of Needs

Abraham Maslow based his psychology on his studies of healthy and successful people rather than taking the direction of most psychologists and studying illness. He discovered that most, if not all, healthy individuals are motivated toward becoming self-actualized.

My guess is that includes you.

Maslow's model proposes that individuals move up from one level to the next only when the needs of the lower level are satisfied. It is an effective way to look at what motivates people to live the way they live.

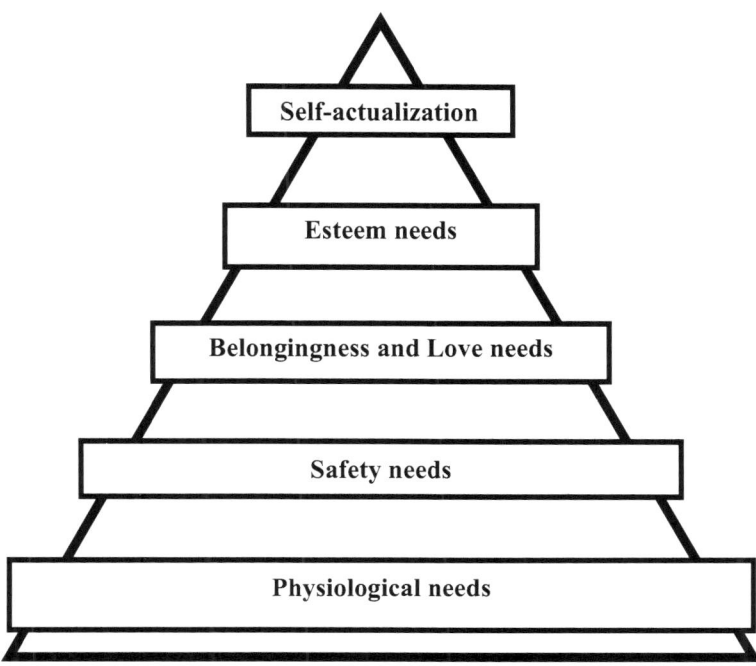

However, people often forego the needs of a so-called lower level in order to pursue the needs of a higher level, sometimes at a huge detrimental cost to their overall well-being.

I believe that prosperity, wealth, happiness, personal fulfillment and self-actualization are achieved when a satisfying balance of all aspects of your beingness is achieved. I define those five aspects as being material, physical, emotional, mental and spiritual.

Let's take a quick look at how Maslow defines each of his five areas...

Physiological Needs: breath, water, food, shelter, sex.

Safety Needs: physical safety, physical health, financial security.

Belongingness Needs: friendship, family, sexual intimacy, love.

Esteem Needs: self-respect, confidence, achievement, respect of others.

Self-Actualization: need to learn, explore, discover and create; desire to grow, to transcend self, to contribute to others.

What are your primary motivators?

Other Books by Leslie Fieger
(Available through LeslieFieger.ca)

Awakenings

This book was written to be a bedside reader. It is collection of ideas, insights, tips, tools and techniques that will empower you to realize your dreams. Read one of the short chapters before going to sleep each night and you will be inspired and empowered to create the successful and fulfilling life you both desire and deserve.

The Master Key

This is the third edition of the 1995 bestseller (25,000+ copies). It is a modern, abridged and annotated version of the almost century-old classic self-study course "The Master Key System" that was also referred to as "The Secret of Success". This is a compilation of proven metaphysical principles and time-tested philosophical truths that you can use to produce real life, testable results in your life.

Alexandra's DragonFire

The tale of a teenage girl who, while on vacation in Costa Rica, encounters the mythological dragon named Pythos hidden away in a cave beneath the active volcano, Arenal. Adventures ensue, both physical and metaphysical, as Alexandra explores the splendors of Costa Rica with her travel writer-parents and as Pythos takes Alex on an even more exciting adventure... the exploration of the mysteries of the meaning and purpose of life. A story of magic and myth, rainforests and rainbows, walking in cloud forests and flying in the clouds, quetzals and quests, tea parties and tempests, and so much more. Come explore with Alex as she discovers the wonders and beauties of Costa Rica and as she, at the same time, also discovers the even more beautiful and wondrous inner landscapes of heart and mind.

The DELFIN Trilogy

The world renowned DELFIN Trilogy has been called "the most comprehensive and effective personal empowerment product ever created".

Book One: The Initiation will enable you to take control over your physical, mental, emotional, and spiritual well being and destiny. Become a creator of the circumstances of your life instead of remaining in the common condition of most of mankind, which is being a creature of circumstance. It is your guide to achieving personal wisdom and finding your life's purpose.

Book Two: The Journey explains that life is a process... a journey. Each of the twelve chapters contain perspectives and techniques which empower you to decide for yourself who you are, where you are at this moment, why you are here, and to what purpose you journey through life. Once you have a clear understanding of those important questions you will achieve the clarity, motivation and inspiration to be an active and joyous participant in your personal journey. The application of your own awareness creates your own road map to success and happiness.

Book Three: The Quest deals with the nature of reality, creation, and transmutation. It contains the keys you will need to unlock your potential to become the master of your own destiny -- to be able to define your own reality, to create your own happiness and fulfillment, to transform into what you have been designed to become.

All three books of The DELFIN Trilogy are augmented by supplemental MP3 audio files. For more information, go to LeslieFieger.ca

Live Events with Leslie Fieger

Leslie is known around the world for empowering the people who attend his talks and seminars. He has educated, motivated and inspired thousands. His unique blend of philosophical knowledge, metaphysical insights and down-to-earth explanations spiced with humor make it possible for all who attend his live events to begin immediately to produce dramatic positive changes in their lives.

"I have worked personally with most of the big names in personal development. Nobody, but nobody, explains the practical relationship between the metaphysical and the physical, the spiritual and the material, better than Leslie Fieger. If you truly want to have success and happiness in your life, you'd be wise to heed his work." ~ Hugh Jeffries

For information on places and dates of his speaking events, or to book Leslie for private functions, go to LeslieFieger.ca

**Become what you need to be
in order to
Enact what needs to be done
in order to
Attain what you desire to have.**

Always remember that you do deserve
to be the success you desire.

Become an envisioneer.

Printed in Great Britain
by Amazon